SMART DEVICES

Carol Rumens was born in Forest Hill, South London, in 1944. She began writing music reviews for the local press when she was sixteen, and her various jobs include the Northern Arts Fellowship, and writer in residence at Queen's University Belfast, University College Cork and the University of Stockholm. She began writing music reviews for the local press when she was sixteen. She has held various literary posts, including the Northern Art Fellowship, and poetry residencies located at Queen's University Belfast, University College Cork, Stockholm University and the Harvard Centre for Hellenic Studies, Nafplio. Rumens has published twenty poetry collections, the latest of which is *The Mixed Urn* (Sheep Meadow Press, 2019). She is a Fellow of the Royal Society of Literature, and Visiting Professor of Creative Writing at the University of Bangor, Gwynedd.

SMART DEVICES

52 Poems from *The Guardian*

'Poem of the Week'

selected and reviewed by

CAROL RUMENS

CARCANET

First published in Great Britain in 2019 by
Carcanet
Alliance House, 30 Cross Street
Manchester M2 7AQ
www.carcanet.co.uk

See pp. 236–8 for details.

A CIP catalogue record for this book is
available from the British Library.
ISBN 978 1 78410 779 6

Book design by Andrew Latimer
Printed in Great Britain by SRP Ltd, Exeter, Devon

FSC www.fsc.org MIX Paper from responsible sources FSC® C014540

The publisher acknowledges financial
assistance from Arts Council England.

Supported using public funding by
ARTS COUNCIL
ENGLAND

CONTENTS

IN MEMORY OF YURIJ DROBYSHEV

1932 – 2015

Your shadow, once light,
Over the calendar of years the years re-write.

SMART DEVICES

INTRODUCTION

This anthology steals its title from the digital technology where, not so many years ago, the concept of the 'Books Blog' was unheard of. But the phrase is intended to set up an antithesis. Poems, which fundamentally rely on technology no more complex than human voices and senses, are devices of a different existential order. Their slow connections take us farther and deeper into human *being*.

As a metaphorical vehicle, the mechanical carries some of poetry's structural attributes. William Carlos Williams famously declared in *The Wedge*, 'A poem is a small (or large) machine made of words. When I say there's nothing sentimental about a poem I mean that there can be no part, as in any other machine, that is redundant.' I prefer to see each poem as a more flexible implement, a miniature neo-cortex – that super-connective, multi-layered smartest device of the mammalian brain. As for redundancy, the poet's task is to convince us that no word is redundant, however wildly plucked. For some advanced readers, metaphor is dead as the exclamation-mark (see the latter bouncing back in Frank Ormsby's poem 'Fireflies' (p.231). But Williams's emphasis on language is important. The poem's external machinery is verbal; its wordy devices – line and stanza, figure and image – compel readers' focus towards language itself.

The 'web-log' is essentially a short form, and, in the case of the *Guardian* 'Poem of the Week', both the prose review (the 'blog') and the poem are expected to add up to an optimal 800 words, although a little leniency prevails. I usually choose published work, encountered first in print and the sweet idleness of the days spent reading for pleasure. While the online poems cover a wide range of historical periods, the fifty-two poems in *Smart Devices*, representing a year's worth of work, but no particular year, are all contemporary. Some have seasonal references, and my arrangement hints at the traditional, newly beleaguered arc of the turning year. That's the extent of the 'agenda'. I've represented a small fraction of the contemporary work featured over the years. Maybe another day I'd have made different choices. The hundreds of equally worthwhile poems excluded can easily be tracked down online in the *Guardian*'s 'Poem of the Week' archive.

All the poems featured during twelve-plus years of 'Poem of the Week' will have made the first move towards attracting my attention, will have stirred or startled me, pleasingly puzzled or simply pleased me, shown me language at its most precise, or conducted a survey of its imprecisions. The poem will have convinced me the voice it sounds in my head is authentic and trustworthy. Importantly, it will have compelled me to write something, not a poem, as I'd prefer, but a review. If it interests me, I'll believe I have something interesting to say about it.

I don't discount a poem's 'message'. Politics and eco-politics play a part in my choice. Sermons have limited appeal, even when eloquently preached, but I like a poem to express a certain grounded idealism and, however questioningly, the sense that an objective truth exists. 'Sacred' would seem a dodgy word, but, for a humanist, it invokes not *theos* but *daimon*, the mysterious appearance that is god-*like*. Why do so many contemporary poems enact or narrate transformation, although with humility and caution? The need for a poetry of vision and encounter might be all the more pressing for contemporary culture. Our technological forms of mimesis favour the feel-good epiphany (blue sea, brave goal, beautiful child). The satisfaction of these images, even for their creators, often proves temporary. The uniqueness and complexity of the experience they represent dies in stereotype, unexplored. I believe we all have intensely interesting truths to communicate, and, while not everyone's a poetic genius, the talent for language is beautifully commonplace. Viva the neo-cortex.

The poem on the webpage is surrounded by capitalism's crudest banalities, and, by words alone, out-smarts them. Poems challenge 'marketing content'. They evade the deductions of surveillance, the super-swift predatory algorithms which invade our imaginations and Midas them into money. I like poems that grab the digital language (which is rich and fascinating) and pin it on an intellectual and moral dissecting table, as does Zohar Atkins's 'The Oy of the Poyem: 28 Lessons in non-Mastery'. Siobhan Campbell's 'Origin of the Mimeo' tackles a now-obsolete smart device with potent political effect. Poems love new language, but only make it significant when they press it into the service of bigger human stories.

There are advantages to the digital platform, of course. Online reviews don't have to be lightweight; they can gain substance from hyperlinks that open magic boxes of reference and cross-reference, and demolish the immigration laws that divide disciplines. But what's really important is the democratised interaction enabled between the contributing journalist and the readers who post comments 'below-the-line'. These conversations are the main factor in the success of the 'Poem of the Week' blog, and the reason I still love doing it and taking part in it.

I inherited it in October 2007 from its gifted founding-editor, Sarah Crown. My first choice, a recommendation from a Welsh colleague, was the late Iwan Lloyd's 'Far Rockaway' translated by Robert Minhinnick. I won't easily forget the horror I felt on reading the tagline:

> In order to prevent 'Poem of the Week' from going the way of all flesh I'm taking the reins. This week's poem is a dreamy choice to chime with National Poetry Day.

I shuddered, not only at the clichés, but the authoritarian sound of 'I'm taking the reins'. There were eleven comments that first week, and they were generous, despite the 'positioning'. In subsequent weeks, though, while the number of commentators increased, challenges were delivered. 'My poem of the week this isn't', one poster wrote of a subsequent choice, and so I had to learn that the poem often wouldn't be as loved as I thought it deserved, or loved at all. Suggestions that I was involved in exchanges of favours, including accepting payment from publishers, were more infuriating. They were, are, always will be completely baseless. I answered back, not always politely.

The blog increased steadily in popularity. The number of comments could hit 300 or more, but at that point, there was much 'off-topic' chit-chat and argument. At the time of writing, in summer 2019, they have settled at around 150. The discussion is sharp, eloquent, focused, and relatively troll-free, but not, I'm grudgingly glad to say, unquestioningly approving.

Sometimes, we laugh. Sometimes, we're cruel. A comment might seem too jokey to be mean, and sometimes it's too mean to be jokey. When Jane Yeh's wonderful poem, 'Musk Ox', was derided in two words, 'boll-ox', or when the poem from Jon lee Keoh *Steep Tea* generated the complaint, '…another week of feeble tea', the word-play didn't make the unpleasantness palatable. Re-reading comments like these, and far worse, I still feel the jab in the guts the poet may have felt. But word-play of the more neutral variety is a delight of the blog: the posters are very good at it, whether pointing out the fact that 'painkiller' contains the word 'ink' or suggesting 'Fake Muse / Is worse than / Fake News'. Sometimes people post parodies, imitations or simply poems of their own. I've done it myself.

A critical riposte that rhymes has mnemonic qualities: 'Roses are red, / Violets are blue. /Rhyming is hard, / Meter is, also.' The latter was meant as a joke, but the most frequently posted serious criticism of contemporary poems is that they're 'chopped-up prose'. Possible answers have included searching out the hidden rhythms or assonantal qualities of the work, blaming the Americans, or asking 'Why does it matter?'

In the past, a poet sometimes contributed to the interpretation of his or her work (or joined in a quarrel about it) That tradition declined. If a poster's poem is chosen, as happens, because many of the posters are serious poets in their own right, the poet tactfully withdraws. Still, I am sure that most glance at what's said. It would be foolish not to, when there are so many devoted acts of close reading and analysis below-the-line.

I hope readers will follow the links included at the foot of each article. Close-reading the poem in question is only a part of what happens. For instance, during a somewhat tedious discussion of the identity of the new wife and former wife in Miriam Nash's 'the Walking Father Blues' (p xxx), the issue of poetic mentoring arose. The question of whether poets can learn to write poetry is always a hot one. This time it sparked an exceptionally well-argued debate.

A week's discussion can be a swirl of hostilities or a marvellous act of shared, collaborative reading. It can be both, where the hostility is backed by good arguement. In the potw community everyone may teach, everyone may learn. It has its brilliant mavericks and blow-ins (I am grateful for those who seem to fall out of the sky with a splash of sunlight, or drop of icy rain) and a fine core of residents. It discloses friendly couples and habitual sparring partners. It has welcomed newcomers and mourned deaths.

Gathered in a compact space like this anthology, poems can be trusted to interact. The ones I selected in my chancy way started to converse intertextually almost without my noticing.

I'll leave the subtler connections for readers to discern: at the simplest level, subject-matter, ornithology has established a nest or two: the post-romantic nightingale (Langley, Burrows), the undying swan (Lambeth, Willson), the Jamaican blackbird (Binta-Breeze).

More frequently than gods and goddesses, allegorical animals reveal contemporary *us* to our contemporary selves. Horta's wolf, Yeh's musk-ox may be challenged, or simply balanced, by the less-anthropomorphised species (Forshaw's Tasmanian Tiger, Capildeo's dog). Today's poet is increasingly an ecologist. A newly responsible pastoral records and names as though conservation itself were part of aesthetic response: sometimes, this pastoral raises its voice. John Kinsella's 'Chainsaw' for example blazes invective. The bird-watchers in Judith Willson's 'A Bone Flute' raise their phones to photograph the swans, but the picture the poet takes transcends the contemporary moment. Her secular epiphany is connected not to an intimation of immortality but to a swathe of past, present and, implicitly, future time. Ross Cogan's 'Lapstrake' is ostensibly about a technique of boat design; it also unpeels the layers of awareness and empathy which make up 'the best' of the good human self.

A poem is more phone-call than smart-phone. We don't respond unless we feel its voice moving, metabolising, inside us. There's much to be said about a poem, but where it meets us most radically may be where our words fail us. One of the reasons I originally accepted the commission was to find out what makes an effective poem, or, more accurately, what I thought makes an effective poem, and how I could say that. Editing the blogs for print publication, I've again tried to refine my critical focus, and justify my heart's affections

The essential quality of smart devices is that they connect to each other without proximity or affiliation. In the popular stereotype of the Internet of Things, toaster speaks unto refrigerator. Poems equally distinct connect across tracts of space and time. Short lyric poems, the microcosmic expression of a particular language combed into personal, provincial dialect, combine as a macrocosm, a borderless epic, inclusive and anti-canonical. As more and more voices, previously marginalised, claim their space of utterance, they make the big story of poetry in English immensely vibrant. *Smart Devices* reflects the beginnings of this radical global renaissance.

There is a good deal of simple generosity in the air around the blog: that of the unpaid poets, the publishers, and, not least, the *Guardian*'s poetry-friendly sub-editors. The 'posters' remain the stars of the discourse, contributing a vigorous range of insight, wit, bullshit and scholarship. Poems, poets and poetry-commentators might not be smart enough, or sufficiently heard, to contribute to our spoiled planet's redemption, but it still forms the sharpest seeing-feeling-knowing machine we currently have. The astonishing linguistic integrations which are poems, are also ourselves, and therefore give us cause for hope.

HOWARD ALTMANN

The Lake of Memories

Voices sit
like broken chairs
in a room.

A room stands
for the ceremony
of impermanence.

Impermanence cracks
the façade
of self.

The self builds
its walls
of healing.

Healing frames
the house
of wounds.

Wounds bridge
darkness and light
over time.

Time winds through
the lake of memories
in frozen tongue.

Howard Altmann grew up in Canada, and has lived for many years in New York City. He writes plays and children's fiction as well as poetry. 'The Lake of Memories' comes from his second collection, *In This House*.

The 'house' for Altmann is rarely a protected personal enclosure: its doors and windows may be open to infiltration by inhuman nature and passing time. It can have more in common with human skin than with bricks-and-mortar: 'A man in a room / is a house in a field' ('Night & Day'). In 'Field', on the other hand, an impregnably shuttered building which 'has sealed its windows and removed its signs', symbolises religion. The day itself is a kind of building in 'Gravity': 'the day's architecture collapses' and the poet finds himself 'walking over words'. In the collection's title poem, the speaker 'can hear a home / knocking at a door / left unlocked for years'. The home finds him in an unhomely but welcoming space, 'at the top of some ridge / [...] / with my walls / building solitude out of trees'. 'The Lake of Memories', too, features a mysteriously potent, almost decipherable lake, its shimmering surface turned by the wind 'into Braille for the half-standing trees'.

The inside-outside fusion in 'The Lake of Memories' is explored through form as well as imagery. The tercets are linked, their stanzaic borders opened by the use of anadiplosis (the repetition of a word at the end of one clause at the beginning of the next). This kind of 'daisy-chain' or 'echo' technique is made more noticeable by the short lines of the tercets. It slows the poem's forward-impulse to a more tentative, step-by-step movement – the manner in which someone might explore an apparently empty house.

'Voices sit / like broken chairs / in a room. // A room stands / for the ceremony of impermanence. // Impermanence cracks / the façade / of self.' Voices that resemble broken chairs are hardly reassuring: they are damaged (by the distortions of time and memory?) and, although they 'sit' in the room as if settled and at home in it, they are evidently not to be relied on. The repetition of solid statements with uncompromising, end-of-line finite verbs (sit, stand, crack) co-exists with a threat of disintegration. Yet the third stanza already makes a concession: the cracking of the 'façade of self' might not be destructive, after all, but the necessary prelude to enhanced consciousness. It seems that a new process is initiated, and concerns the building of 'walls / of healing'. This may primarily be a psychological process, but it also suggests the biochemistry involved in the healing of physical wounds.

The imagery in stanza six, implying that the wounds are historical and their healing long-term, reminded me of a poem nearer the beginning of the collection, in which the speaker recounts, 'When he was a young man / at Auschwitz / my father leapt out of line / for a potato / and was saved by a bell / that never rang. / Sixty years later he stands / in his place / by his mother's tomb – / the only tomb – containing / his hunger for memory' ('History'). While 'The Lake of Memories' stands by itself, it may reprise that earlier memory-infused narrative in compressed, symbolic form.

The process implied in the last tercet is a strange combination of movement and stasis: 'Time winds through / the lake of memories / in frozen tongue.' The phrase 'frozen tongue' has many metaphorical overtones: unsatisfied or thwarted hunger, a language no longer communicative, perhaps no longer spoken, a decision not to speak. There's a paradox in the idea that such a tongue can 'wind through' the lake, somehow alive despite its frozenness. But the future nonetheless seems to have been brought into being by the transformative concept of the wounds forming a bridge.

Wounds heal by a complex, gradual process which includes some connective, cellular activity not dissimilar to bridge-building. The scar might be seen as a 'bridge' of skin cells, regenerated, though no longer fully functional as before. Altmann's poem seems to perform in its slow-paced repetitions and accumulating metaphors a similar operation. The 'ceremony of impermanence' is not only destructive: time's 'frozen tongue' itself may form a secret bridge.

Despite the poem's brevity and economy, and the fact that it continues to inhabit, through the repeated symbols of wounds and healing, a physical enclosure, the sense of surrounding open space contributes a frail atmosphere of hope. It reminds us that the poet's formative years were spent in Canada. The lake is 'the lake of memories', and, like the other natural imagery in Altmann's poems, it's metaphorically liberating, but never simply metaphorical.

https://www.theguardian.com/books/booksblog/2016/dec/05/poem-of-the-week-the-lake-of-memories-by-howard-altmann

PETER DIDSBURY

A Fire Shared

This evening I have spent
in the Irishwoman's room.
A fire shared is a fire cheaper.

A twelvemonth since
I knew her not at all.
Our hearths were crowded then
but now it is fitting
that one of them bides cold.
A fire shared is a fire cheaper by far.

She has enough English now
for January tales
of our slavering *bargeist*
which stalks these dark flagged yards
intent on the taking of children.
She would not have understood a year ago.

A year ago her English was just enough
for blessing or cursing,
to ask the price of bread
or directions to a pump.
But now a fire shared
is a fine instructive tutor.

She has enough English now
to match my *bargeists* and goblins
with *pookas* and suchlike,
and I find I have learned what these are,
from many a night
spent sharing and cheapening fire.

A twelvemonth ago I would not have known
the Irish for 'sorrow', 'cholera', 'children',
or who stood by me at the same wide grave-mouth
as we wept after each of our fashions.
But now I know these things,
which are things I have learned
in the school of the ruined hearth,
which is held in both our rooms,
where a fire shared
is the cheapest fire of all.

The Hull-based poet and archaeologist Peter Didsbury brings an informed historical imagination to his writing. At the same time, he is often a poet of borderless transition – between lyric and narrative, comedy and tragedy, fantastic and realistic.

'A Fire Shared' recalls the old proverb, 'A trouble shared is a trouble halved', traditionally abbreviated to 'A trouble shared'. Plenty of trouble has afflicted both characters in the poem, and it's what connects them across different cultures. The wry, unsentimental variations played on the theme of 'a fire shared' ('A fire shared is a fire cheaper', etc.) form a refrain which has a slightly teasing, evasive quality. Subtle changes may imply a building intimacy between the couple, ('many a night / spent sharing and cheapening fire') and draw us into the hearth-side of the night they've narrowly escaped.

Many Irish immigrants arrived in the port city of Hull during the nineteenth century. In the essay that accompanied the poem's first publication in *Poetry Ireland* 78, Didsbury notes that, during the summer cholera epidemic of 1849, 'upwards of two thousand people perished in three months'. He quotes a report by a clergyman of the time, describing how the Irish women would fling themselves onto the graves and 'howl out, in their native tongue, the 'death wail'. The echo of this 'keen' (Irish – 'caoine'), softened by the passage of time and the sharing of friendship, can perhaps be picked up in the cadences of the poem's refrain.

The linguistic process detailed in stanzas 3 – 5 foreshadows an eventual loss of language for the Irishwoman. Her estrangement from English has been modified... 'a fire shared / is a fine instructive tutor'. She will become fluent in English and, implicitly, the dominant language will obliterate her own. But at this early stage of assimilation, the learning is two-way, and delicately balanced between the conversationalists.

In bridging languages, the speaker and the woman have used local myths which relate to the snatching of children, and are therefore relevant to their particular tragedies. Their 'bonding', it's implied, is a shared humanity deeper than linguistic and cultural sharing. Mutual compassion forms a sturdy foundation for the ultimately fiery politics of the poem.

There may be an erotic dimension to the narrative. The sharing of fire could indicate sexual or romantic excitement, and the economy of sharing which the poem praises might suggest marriage. The speaker could be of either gender, but I imagine a male speaker, perhaps a clergyman or teacher, who has fallen on hard times. He has offered help, and sitting down at the Irish woman's hearth, perhaps he goes beyond the faintly scholarly pleasures of exchanging folk-tales and words, and both progress beyond the sharing of grief to pleasure.

Whoever the speaker is, male or female, fish-wife or schoolmaster, there is nothing literary in the voice. The language is beautifully plain and simple, with its unforced touches of dialect. The inversion of the opening sentence ('This evening I have spent / in the Irishwoman's room') surprises us into attention. Does it have a faintly Hibernian-English flavour? And what about 'A twelvemonth since / I knew her not at all'? That fine, homely verb, 'bides', as in 'bides cold', belongs to Old English, of course ('abidan'). These little quirks of idiom not only give the poem force and freshness: they seem to suggest the assimilations and losses that the speakers are already sharing.

The narrative moves forward cumulatively, almost like a folk-tale, quietly building up the background detail. It's hard not to seem over-expository when imparting information in a monologue. This poem never seems so. Description is minimal but essential. 'Dark flagged yards' evokes an entire neighbourhood; the isolate words, 'sorrow', 'cholera', 'children', give us the whole emotional and narrative core. So we discover that these two people have met unknowingly before, at the graveside, where they expressed their grief in such different ways they did not realise that it was essentially the same grief.

Shakespeare's 'Sweet are the uses of adversity' is another 'saying' the poem calls to mind, and to which it give edge. We understand that the characters have somehow learned to be generous, patient and unaffected with one another. We can almost hear them, muttering quietly like the fire. But the sweetness is bitter, too, and hard lessons learned 'in the school of the ruined hearth, / which is held in both our rooms'.

https://www.theguardian.com/books/booksblog/2010/jun/28/ poem-week-fire-shared-didsbury

KAREN McCARTHY WOOLF

Outside

under the arcade
and the floor-length glass shop front:
a green pop-up dome

flanked by a Burberry
suitcase and a sleeping-bag

a makeshift shelter
for Sai from Stratford
with time to invest

in a four-day queue – he's first
in line for an iPhone 6s

no-one moves him on
or threatens arrest
as it's not about where

but why you pitch your tent

Karen McCarthy Woolf's collection, *Seasonal Disturbances,* is a delicately interlocked, formally experimental, almost origami-like collection of poems and sequences. Among the highlights is a set of found sonnets, 'The Science of Life', drawn from the eponymous 1931 encyclopaedia, and responding to 'eXXpedition', an all-women sailing voyage investigating the effects of micro-plastic pollution. There's also a 'disrupted zuihitsu' threading through the collection like a partly-subterranean river, and work in a glosa-like form, invented and named by the poet, *coupling.* For all its internationalism, McCarthy Woolf's poetry engages with the local and personal. Reading *Seasonal Disturbances* is like picking up a map of her home-city, London, and unfolding a new map of the world. It seems vandal-ish to pick it apart, but there are some poems which stand singly, forming little pools of calm in the interwoven currents, and 'Outside' is one of them.

The poem is tactically simple, depicting a young man queuing overnight to buy a smartphone, and noticing his immunity to the harassment usually inflicted on rough sleepers. The tone is resolutely objective, though rising at the end to a wry, summary aphorism.

Brief cultural signifiers position 'Sai from Stratford', a young city-type, 'with time to invest // in a four-day queue'. In fact, he's first in the queue, which indicates a certain heroism, or at least determination, in the pursuit of a perhaps not-altogether secure personal 'status'. The repeated 's' sounds in stanza 3 onwards (invest, first, 6s, arrest) rustle like the notes he probably doesn't carry.

Sai's designer (Burberry) suitcase, lodged outside the 'green pop up dome' advertises his affluence and therefore guarantees his rights of residence on London's (or any Western city's) 'charter'd streets'. He is covered by that charter, in fact. Another person would be designated by law a vagrant or trespasser but he's a wealthy consumer. And so he's left alone.

I had to do some research on the iPhone 6s, being of the generation for whom '6s' meant the very decent childhood sum of 'six shillings'. The treasure Sai covets boasts 3D Touch ('the next generation of Multi Touch') and a 12 megapixel iSight camera, with Live Photos and Retina Flash. It opens up 'new possibilities for how you interact with your content'.

As its name suggests, the iPhone's focus is egocentric. It wraps up our brains in a feedback loop no analogue device could achieve. It presents a miniature world, and announces you the emperor. It can sell you anything. It lets you delete all the rough sleepers from the streets.

Sai (pronounced Sah-yee) is a significant name, meaning 'saint, master or lord in Sindhi and Marathi'. In naming her protagonist Sai, McCarthy Woolf has evoked the sacrosanct, suggesting the possession of so-called 'iconic' goods confers nearly godlike power. The word literally means 'shade' and it was once a 'poetic way' of referring to the Sufi mystics, associating them with 'the protective and influential'. Sai from Stratford may have become an outsider to his own tradition. But he is still protected, even when queuing for four days outside 'the floor-length glass shop front', because, in terms of Western values, he is an insider.

'[I]t's not about where // but why you pitch your tent.' The poem makes its point and stops. A writer of less subtlety than McCarthy Woolf, wishing to make a similar point, might have chosen to depict a vagrant in all his or her misery, or to contrast the two urban figures, neighbours but worlds apart, sleeping out on a city street. McCarthy Woolf zones in on the more fortunate figure. But she also holds back. No blame attaches to him for buying into the values that surround him.

Society isn't directly blamed, either. The poem seems to skip sideways into neutrality: 'no-one moves him on', 'it's not about'. Authority remains un-named, as if part of the air people breathe. In its offhand way, it's a frightening poem, a reminder that there are unwritten rules made by unnamed legislators, obeyed unintentionally. How can someone be outside their own society? How can anyone who makes it work for themselves be held responsible for those for whom it doesn't work? The poem slips past, leaving a guilty shadow. We look down and see the shadow's our own.

https://www.theguardian.com/books/booksblog/2017/dec/25/poem-of-the-week-outside-by-karen-mccarthy-woolf

FRED D'AGUIAR

Boy Soldier

What a smile! One large lamp for a face,
smaller lanterns where skin stretches over
bones waiting for muscle, body all angles.

His Kalashnikov fires at each moving
thing before he knows what he drags
down. He halts movement of every
kind and fails to weigh whom he stops

dead or maims, his bullets
like jabs thrown before the thought
to throw them, involuntary shudders
when someone, somewhere, steps over

his shallow, unmarked, mass grave.
But his smile remains undimmed,
inviting, not knowing what hit him,
what snuffs out the wicks in his eyes.

Except that he moves and a face just like
his figures like him to stop all action
with a flick of finger on the trigger.

A prolific, many-talented explorer of literary genres including drama, prose fiction and the verse-novel, Fred D'Aguiar fuses both contemporary and traditional expectations of the poet's role. A sense of public accountability frequently grounds and enlarges his interpretation of the lyric poem.

From his recent collection, *The Rose of Toulouse,* the jagged song of lost innocence, 'Boy Soldier', has some of the directness and moral indignation we associate with William Blake. The particular hostilities in which the child is caught are not named or located: the boy portrayed couldn't name them. He is the universal child-soldier, all his unrealised childhood in his unknowing smile.

Instantly visual, the tercet brings the reader straight into contact with him, and asserts the speaker's surprise and empathy: 'What a smile!' A detached, almost 'Martian School' style of observation braces the fatherly tenderness. As for that older generation of poet-reporters, compassion expresses itself largely through watchful, ego-free attention to the subject.

The smile of the boy soldier summons a romantic convention of child photography, and immediately complicates it, moving from the 'large lamp' of the face to the bony 'lanterns' of the skinny, under-nourished, unformed body, 'waiting for muscle'. The pathos of that 'waiting' will become apparent in the prophetic fourth stanza. Meanwhile, after the establishing close-up, a cleverly transitional phrase, 'body all angles', evokes not only the physique but the rapidity of movement as the boy goes into action.

The poem's rhythm is angular, too, despite its stanzaic symmetry, with curtly enjambed lines jutting through the flow of the syntax, and occasional abbreviation of the syntax itself. Dramatic, cliff-hanger pauses occur at many of the line-endings ('moving / thing', 'drags / down', etc.) culminating in the cross-stanza breaking of 'stops // dead'. By separating two elements of an ordinary-enough verbal phrase, the poet slows the action and achieves compression. The boy 'stops // dead' his unknown victim, and the victim himself stops, and falls dead, in slower motion. But, of course, the sentence, like the boy, carries on. The point is that the child has not thought about his target: he shoots at whatever moves and 'fails to weigh whom he stops // dead *or maims*' (my italics). Several verbs in the poem suggest hunting, and an awkward, painful, inefficient 'kill'. That the bullets are compared to 'jabs thrown…' recalls the more playful sport a normally raised boy might enjoy, like boxing.

The boy's failure to weigh things up is the result of carrying too much adult weight, metaphorically and literally: 'His Kalashnikov fires at each moving / thing.' The gun seems bigger than him, with a will of its own. Recruited by force, given brutal training, and possibly drugged, he has been reduced to a small, disposable set of reflexes.

A novelistic device now fast-forwards the narrative, revealing what will happen to the boy, and others like him. His body itself registers this in the 'involuntary shudders / when someone, somewhere, steps over // his shallow, unmarked, mass grave'. The superstition is commonplace, but used to striking effect: it's one of the moments when we see clearly the boy's own vulnerability, and the vulnerability of all war-used bodies, shuddering involuntarily as they are brought down.

In stanza 4 we are witnessing his death, perhaps, like him, not realising it at first because 'his smile remains undimmed, inviting'. Again, an ordinary colloquialism is made to resonate: this child truly doesn't know what has hit him. The opening 'lamp' metaphor is resumed with poignant visual clarity: 'not knowing… / what snuffs out the wicks in his eyes'.

At this point the boldest of the pauses occurs. A full-stop and a stanza break appear to terminate the action at the end of the 4th stanza. But the poem goes on and allows us to identify the new figure. The presence of this assailant gains emphasis by being cordoned off, though the clause qualifies the 'not knowing' of the preceding stanza. 'Except that he moves' assigns a gender to the unknown mover: he is, of course, another boy-soldier.

Now it's as if the speaker and the first boy-soldier unite in their recognition of the second child's identity. He's like the first child's mirror-image. And because this tercet is itself a mirror-image, reflecting the opening stanza, we might imagine the poem's beginning again, with this other face, smiling largely, this other innocently-lethal Kalashnikov. The implied circularity takes us towards a general sense of war as a cycle of futility, without blurring the particular portrayal – that of a young boy subjected to a form of enslavement. It's estimated that three-quarters of the world's current conflicts recruit children. The boy-soldier is a child of our time, and a child of our silence and shame.

https://www.theguardian.com/books/booksblog/2013/may/27/poem-of-the-week-fred-d-aguiar

RUTH FAINLIGHT

The Coloration of Feathers

For glory and brilliance, the colours of feathers
are unsurpassed. Yet the pigments which produce
those shades are few. Some (called subjective
or optical colours) are illusions formed
by the quills' pattern and its achromatic,
horny surface. Is other creatures' vision
of them different, paler or darker, than ours?

Melanin, from blood-plasma or haemoglobin,
makes black, brown and grey; turacin, which fades
when wet, will flush to purple. Darwin wrote
that natives of the Amazonian region
feed fatty fish to green parrots so the lipochromes
will streak them red and yellow (the sacred
tints of royal Inca's feather garments).

Prismatic and metallic tones: blue, gold
and glossy black, are the structural colours.
Only the white lacks underlying pigment.
The evolution of vivid plumage began with
the struggle to win a mate. But the drab hues
of survivors disturb: such complex beauty
unnecessary after that triumph.

St Valentine's Day, now imminent, is the fabled wedding day of the birds. The origins of the fable are often attributed to Geoffrey Chaucer's 'dream-vision' poem, *Parliament of Fowls*. This narrative is thought to have been composed in honour of the marriage of Richard II and Anne of Bohemia; however, in Chaucer's tale, the central love-match doesn't quite happen.

Among the flocks of soulmate-seeking birds, three male eagles are vying for a single hen. 'Nature' advises the hen to choose the royal eagle, but the hen requests a year's postponement to think things over, and, in addition, asks that the choice should ultimately be hers alone. Dame Nature obligingly grants these wishes. Meanwhile, all the other birds are allotted their perfect partners, and burst into song. The poet-narrator wakes up, already looking forward to his next dream.

Contemporary poems about birds are numerous, and the challenge is to resist sentimentality and fabulation, while capturing the alien magic. The American-born poet, Ruth Fainlight, has chosen not to write about a particular species, but to explore the chemistry of plumage in 'The Coloration of Feathers'. The poem appears in her 2002 Bloodaxe collection, *Burning Wire*, a rich-textured work featuring flowers, clothes, pictures, 'Peruvian Views' and feathers. The 'feather' poems originally forming the text of an art-book, with mezzo-tints by Judith Rothchild (Édition Verdigri, Octon, France), are still enticingly visual by themselves.

Varied registers of language operate in 'The Coloration of Feathers'. The formal definition is one of them, and in fact the three stanzas, consisting of mostly run-on lines, look a little like blocks of text in an encyclopaedia. That it would be an old-fashioned kind of encyclopaedia, the entries reflecting the compiler's personal engagement with the topic, is suggested by the emotive first sentence, with its breathlessly evaluative words like 'glory', 'brilliance', 'unsurpassed'. A more detached and specialised register contributes textbook phrases and words: 'subjective / or optical colours', 'achromatic'. Another voice, possibly the poet's own, interrupts the explanations with its curiosity about 'other creatures' vision'. This question itself is linked to the assertion that some colours are illusory. Philosophical depths open up. Are colours real, differently real to different eyes, or non-existent without an observer?

The main perspective on the plumage-colours is that of the human eye. But the poem prompted me to glance at some research on avian vision and I was intrigued to discover that some species can see colours belonging to the ultraviolet part of the spectrum – handy for insect-detection, of course, and adding still more gorgeous glamour to the male bird's wardrobe, if only in the eyes of rivals and girl-friends.

Fainlight's vocabulary shows the reader new verbal colours. Facts enrich poems (even if we don't go to poems for facts): scientific jargon can be an aesthetic resource. When absorbed into the overall verbal texture, as here, those articulated, polysyllabic juggernauts ('achromatic', 'haemoglobin'), freighted with their Greek or Latin origins, provide not only precision of meaning but intense visual and aural pleasure.

The anecdote in stanza 2, recorded by Darwin, concerns a low-tech kind of genetic engineering. (Darwin's writing seems a particularly poet-friendly source of ideas: see Anne Stevenson's 'The Miracle of the Bees and the Foxgloves', p.189). For Fainlight, the story about the Amazonian parrots connects with South American themes elsewhere in her collection, and raises an issue about the human control of other species, pertinent to the end of this particular poem.

Before we reach that moment of disturbance, there's a steely shimmer of 'prismatic and metallic tones' to detain us. The emphatic colour-contrasts, 'blue, gold…glossy black' ('the structural colours') suggest birds familiar to northern European gardens: starlings, magpies, jays, crows, goldfinches.

Although un-named (the only birds the poet names are the green parrots) these species are given life and movement by coruscating adjectives..

Near-synonyms found for the word 'colour' encompass 'shades', 'tints', 'tones', 'hues', each having a different sound and, indeed, a slightly different coloration. If words have colours, what colour is 'coloration'? Does the English or American spelling of 'colour' make a difference to our perception of the word's meaning? There's puzzle as well as dazzle in this intriguing poem.

Finally, the subjective voice addresses a paradox: the successful species tend to have 'drab hues' as if the 'complex beauty' they no longer need to exhibit was simply an evolutionary phase. One reason the drab species are 'survivors' may, of course, be due to their lack of visibility to predators outweighing their mating disadvantage. But even that could generate a politically disturbing thought. To the poet, a child of émigré ancestors, it may suggest populations living subterranean lives under grim regimes that suppress diversity and creative energy, or being obliged to lie low and blend into unwelcoming places of refuge. Or perhaps the view Fainlight wants us to glimpse is of a dystopian future, a time when organisms like us are wholly functional and machine-like. Will artistic activity become our own redundant plumage one cybernetic day? The poem, after all its bright and sensuous vitality, leaves us in a lengthening shadow.

https://www.theguardian.com/books/2012/feb/13/ poem-of-the-week-ruth-fainlight

JUDITH WILSON

A Bone Flute

made from the radius bone of a Whooper Swan wing,
c. 40,000 years ago

Swans flying in across the lagoon at dusk, muscled as horses;
sky filling with bells. The swans dip and rock, lanterns

on the grey water and we raise our phones' small lamps
as if we should honour the messengers returning at nightfall

to patient souls who stand beside cars with their children
in bright winter coats holding bags of grain,

provisioned for a journey. The swans lift their necks,
open the great doors of their wings. Our faces are fading

behind our white breath; a flute's seven feathery notes
still dissolving on the air. Mothers or sisters

walking towards us, hold out their hands.
They will sit with us, watch the hours swing round,

skeins streaming north. Soon the year's sharp light
will sing in the bone. Soon they will take what they came for.

The Whooper Swan (*Cygnus cygnus*) is a winter migrant from Iceland, resident in the British Isles and Ireland between November and March. Judith Willson's poem, from her fine debut collection, *Crossing the Mirror Line*, begins with the dramatic scene of the birds' arrival. Its opening couplet packs the description in tightly, the arresting image of these large birds, 'muscled as horses', mutating to one which adds sound effects. Bells, though, are not pure sonority: they are solid, sky-lit, space-packing, highly distinctive shapes, and so suggest an enriching, de-familiarising visual metaphor.

The swans' mass-landing is clean and contained as the verbs, 'dip' and 'rock'. On the quiet grey water, they morph rather magically into lanterns. Lantern light, diffuse and ancient, is qualitatively different from the keener glow of the 'phones' small lamps'. The kinship of the two words, lamp and lantern, delicately heightens their distinction, an important one for the poem's retreat into pre-history.

Sound is at least as important to the poem as image. The name 'Whooper' is suggestive, of course, but how realistic is it as onomatopoeia? In a poem in *Goats Milk*, Frank Ormsby describes it as 'a dolorous whomp'. That's certainly evocative of some of the lower-pitched Whooper notes. The birds have quite a range of pitch: the poet does well in not attempting to be 'tweet-of-the-day' specific. Her soundscape is subtler and altogether stranger.

Meanwhile, the narrative continues on its almost-realist way. People have gathered to welcome the swans (or perhaps, as the poster @gardinergreen suggested, to send them well-fed on a further leg of their journey to the Arctic). They have brought their children, and might have driven some distance, 'in bright winter coats holding bags of grain'. That's a wonderfully concrete line, splashing clear vivid colour, Breughel-like, against winter white and grey. There's another, distant Breughel-connection. In Auden's 'Musée des Beaux

Arts', the speaker praises the Old Masters' understanding of 'How, when the aged are reverently, passionately waiting / For the miraculous birth, there always must be / Children who did not specially want it to happen, skating / On a pond at the edge of the wood'. In Willson's poem, another kind of 'miraculous birth' is presented obliquely. It's not simply the advent of the migrant swans. That literal arrival is only part of the whole story, almost a side-track.

Some other order of consciousness is already infiltrating the poem. Filming the birds, it's 'as if we should honour the messengers returning at nightfall // to patient souls'. Are the witnesses cheerful middle-class bird-lovers parked beside a perfectly ordinary lagoon, or shades on the banks of the River Lethe? Are the swans themselves becoming souls? The 'feathery' notes of the bone flute lift the narrative into another time. Dualities of life/death and breath/sound are erased with the image of 'our faces (…) fading // behind our white breath' and the sound of 'a flute's seven feathery notes / still dissolving on the air'.

Bone flutes were among the first musical instruments humans invented. Archaeological investigations at the Hohle Fels cave in the Swabian Jura yielded many. The tune played 'c.40,000 years ago' has yet to vanish. It's so placed that the swans seem to have retreated through 'the great door of their wings'. Encapsulating and distilling all that's left of their hungry, muscly, noisy presence is the sound of the small flute.

Now the realism loosens and the poem becomes more associative. On one level, it might trace the transition of life to art, via death. I find the phrase 'mothers or sisters' particularly mysterious. Are the women swans or people, or swan-people? They seem to have risen from the dead, with an ambiguous offering for the living. They are almost but not quite flesh-and-blood. We don't know if they are the speaker's dead: the casual option of identification ('or') suggests not. The gendering might imply particular demands made by women on women, especially on the woman-artist. Though they'll 'sit with us, watch the hours swing round' they will be overseeing a deepening of winter. The acts of sitting and watching suggest the traditional death-bed, while the 'skeins streaming north' imply the hopeful flight. Once the swans have left, will the mothers and sisters 'take what they came for'? These strange, harsh figures with their outstretched hands seem more dangerously predatory than the swans. But perhaps, like the swans, they simply want to live.

What very definitely happens in the poem is that it gets colder: deathly cold. Any bone in which the 'year's sharp light' can 'sing' must be a bone without flesh or feather. Listen to a recording of the Palaeolithic flute. The instrument was made from a swan's radius. Whether or not it was the source of the poem, it's the very sound of the cold, the thinnest icicle of a not-quite-tuneless tune.

https://www.theguardian.com/books/booksblog/2018/jan/08/ poem-of-the-week-a-bone-flute-by-judith-willson

DENISE RILEY

Death makes dead metaphor revive

Death makes dead metaphor revive,
Turn stiffly bright and strong.
Time that is felt as 'stopped' will freeze
Its to-fro, to-fro song

I parrot under feldspar rock
Sunk into chambered ice.
Language, the spirit of the dead,
May mouth each utterance twice.

Spirit as echo clowns around
In punning repartee
Since each word overhears itself
Laid bare, clairaudiently.

An orphic engine revs but floods
Choked on its ardent weight.
Disjointed anthems dip and bob
Down time's defrosted spate.

Over its pools of greeny melt
The rearing ice will tilt.
To make *rhyme* chime again with *time*,
I sound a curious lilt.

‘The only constant is a commitment to the thing that is song’, Denise Riley said of her poetry in an interview with Shearsman, whose magazine was the first publisher of this week’s poem (issue 97/98). Riley’s new collection, *Say Something Back,* frequently foregrounds song, not least in the major elegiac sequence, *A Part Song*. ‘Death makes dead metaphor revive’, a poem closely related to her prose meditation, *Time Lived Without Its Flow*, demonstrates the mourner’s recovery of time-as-movement through the sounding of ‘a curious lilt’

In the Shearsman interview, Riley mentions the hymns of Isaac Watts. Emily Dickinson’s poems throve on the same stringency, and the description, in line 2 of the poem, of dead metaphor’s capacity to become ‘stiffly bright and strong’, seems particularly to evoke Dickinson’s brilliantly lapidary quatrains.

In *The Language of Metaphors*, the linguist Andrew Goatly defines a dead metaphor as one in which the vehicle has become so remote from the tenor that all that remains is a homonym. He gives the word ‘pupil’ as an example: few of us now recognise there was once a metaphorical connection between the two meanings. Sadly, the tenor (or, as Goatly prefers, ‘topic’) ‘young student’ and the vehicle, ‘an opening in the eye’s iris so as to admit light’ parted company long ago.

Our everyday understanding of the dead metaphor (itself a metaphorical phrase, attributing life and death to a figure of speech) is simply that it has lost its force for some reason, perhaps simply through over-use. The third line offers the clue to what that metaphor may be: ‘Time that is felt as stopped’. This complex passive construction already challenges the cliché, ‘time stopped’. ‘Time… felt as’ acknowledges the subjectivity of the metaphorical interpretation. ‘Time that is… stopped’ could be time as movement halted in its progress, time stoppered, like a bottle of liquid, and time stopped like a musical instrument. All these metaphors are linked but different. The commonest metaphor, time as a stream or river, is well-worn, and dated by its dependence on a view of time as linear, forward movement.) Images of ice and rock revive the 'dead' metaphor of the poem by literalising it: rivers still flow seawards and can still freeze over, whatever new theories of time are advanced, and geological processes still have their psychological counterparts.

The 'song' the poem's first stanza evokes appears to be time's. Its non-linear, pendulum-like 'to-fro, to-fro' motion has halted. As we follow the sentence over the stanza-break we find out that the speaker hopelessly 'parrot(s)' this doomed song. She is located under the feldspar rock, and perhaps even under the frozen river, 'sunk into chambered ice'. This suggests a burial chamber, perhaps, and a voice entombed, repetitive, echoing, punning.

'The souls of the dead are the spirit of language: / You hear them alight inside that spoken thought.' These lines conclude another poem, 'Listening for lost people', and their passion is relived in 'Death makes dead metaphor revive'. The latter poem, I think, is modifying the earlier thought, and saying that while the spirit of the dead is language, the words are spoken by the living, and so the dead are heard, 'clairaudiently', echoing, or seeming to echo, the living voice. 'Clairaudient' is the aural equivalent of 'clairvoyant' and suggests a special receptivity to what is actual, although not generally perceptible.

The notion of echo is at first bitterly, hollowly comic ('I parrot', 'clowns around', 'punning repartee') but later seems productive. It evolves into rhyme, which is more than echo, the disturbing metaphorical turn given by stanza 4 to the Orpheus myth notwithstanding. Time's flow remains awkward, not fully restored: there are non-fluent 'pools of greeny melt' and 'disjointed anthems' suggesting, as well as troubled sounds, the visual detritus of chunks of ice and other remnants breaking up in the churning of a partly thawed river. Ice remains the dominant structure: it still rears and threatens from above, as if from the conscious mind deploring the body's instinctive self-perpetuation.

The poem moves fluently between concrete and abstract. The metaphor, made real by the experience of death, not only revives but becomes fertile and breeds others more intricate and tangible– the feldspar rock, the underground 'chambered ice', the flooded engine: all operate as further stops to the redemptive flow. At the same time, the mineral solidity in this poem strengthens it. Echo and rhyme are demonstrably more than reflexes obeying the banal instruction mourners are given, or may even give themselves, to 'move on'. Rhymes are sometimes antithetical ('weight / spate'): they can demonstrate a process or leap somewhere new ('ice / twice'). To mourn is not only to weep: it's to listen. For the mother grieving for her silenced child, rhyme is reply as well as echo.

https://www.theguardian.com/books/booksblog/2016/jun/13/ poem-of-the-week-death-makes-dead-metaphor-revive-by-denise-riley

ZOHAR ATKINS

The Oy of the Poyem: 28 Exercises in non-Mastery

Click here for 29 reasons
you are not *not* Mark Ruffalo.

Click here for 6 proofs
Buzzfeed is a distraction from the Buzzfeed as such.

Click *next* to receive yourself as a coupon.
Click Play Now to become forever.

Click Incognito Mode to avoid the paywall,
discover 10 myths you thought were facts.

If the font ain't Calypso, switch to Reality.
If Reality ain't high definition,

petition your senator here.
Each day, thousands of innocents

lack yoghurt, political will,
and courage to wear bright clothing.

Coincidence? Each second
you give to thinking

will be matched by 30 minutes
of callousness, regret, and avoidance.

Click here to short your cynicism,
make millions in emerging emotional markets.

In the long-run, even mavericks fall
on one side of the fence, wondering

why they didn't learn Esperanto.
In the short-run we are all unborn.

'That wasn't 28.'
'Nu? So it wasn't 28.'

Zohar Atkins, Rabbi and theologian, is the founding director of Etz Hasadeh and a David Hartman Fellow at the Shalom Hartman Institute of North America. He lives up to his name (Zohar means 'light' in Hebrew and gives its name to a set of mystical commentaries on the Torah). His first collection, *Nineveh*, is an imginative illumination of history, including plenty of 'today' and a little of 'tomorrow'. He's a poet who can happily rhyme 'mystical' with 'listicle'.

Nineveh takes delight in bringing disciplines and dictions together to argue with each other. Incantation and instruction, meditation techniques and the social media, meet in this week's poem, which takes the shape of a parodic 'listicle' – an online article structured as a list and making use of cardinal numbers. An informal Yiddish idiom adds essential colour, homeliness and an ironical shrug. Let's begin with the title, which puts the 'oy' in 'poyem'.

David Robson suggests in an amusing column in the Jewish Chronicle, 'Oy! The Word that Says it All', that 'oy' is a 'Goy proof' word (questionable, I think. No word is anyone-proof!) He explains that 'a thousand Chasidic oys equal one extended Buddhist 'Om-m-m-m' – a nice listicle-style aphorism in the spirt of Akins's poem, adding that 'A single "oy" does justice to almost any crisis and every ecstasy'. It seems that's a thought to hold onto as we read.

'Poyem' carries perhaps an echo of 'payim' from 1 Samuel 13: 21–23 where it represents two-thirds of a shekel of silver, the cost of sword-sharpening. Poetry, and keen speech itself, has a price? At the same time, Atkins is alive to the sheer 'j-oy' of his art, including its significance for meditation. There's an underlying awareness of what poetry can achieve through its own self-examination, and a potential for 'ecstacy' as well as 'crisis' in many of his poems. This one is ultimately a demonstration of the triumph of argument.

Instructions are essential to both digital communications and the spiritual exercise, but the result of the proposed 28, we're told at once, is 'non-mastery'. That's reassuring. The satirical emphasis throughout the poem falls on the commands and the promised 'magical' result, but the couplets suggest some profound logical investigation, as well as being funny. Even the first and simplest stimulates the brain-cells with its double-take double-negative: 'Click here for 29 reasons / you are not *not* Mark Ruffalo.' Ethical and mystical notes enhance the flavour of stanza 3. 'Click *next* to receive yourself as a coupon. / Click Play Now to become forever.' The results of the two clicks seem antithetical at a first glance, but both may represent forms of hubris, one material, the second spiritual.

I mentioned the aphorism earlier: conjuring aphorisms is one of the skills Atkins has brilliantly not *not* mastered. Poetry likes them, readers love them, at least when they're not glib or otherwise unearned. There's an underlying moral seriousness to their playful deployment by Atkins, when they are playful. Sometimes, of course, they're simply serious: 'Each second you give to thinking // will be matched by 30 minutes / of callousness, regret, and avoidance.'

The poem is a fine, bright-witted balancing act. Political anger is evident in the vision of a plague of digitised consumerist ephemera which eventually annihilates conscience. Even when cynicism is overcome, the result is (you) 'make millions in emerging emotional markets'. There is some sad wisdom about mavericks in stanzas 11 and 12. Then the mood lightens, as challenge and discussion take over. The final 'nu' is a shrug and a saving grace.

https://www.theguardian.com/books/booksblog/2019/jun/24/ poem-of-the-week-the-oy-of-the-poyem-by-zohar-atkins

JOHN ASHBERY

Breezeway

Someone said we needed a breezeway
to bark down remnants of super storm Elias jugularly.
Alas it wasn't my call.
I didn't have a call or anything resembling one.
You see I have always been a rather dull-spirited winch.
The days go by and I go with them.
A breeze falls from a nearby tower,
finds no breezeway, goes away
along a mission to supersize red shutters.

Alas if that were only all.
There's the children's belongings to be looked to
if only one can find the direction needed
and stuff like that.
I said we were all homers not homos
but my voice dwindled in the roar of Hurricane Edsel.
We have to live out our precise experimentation.
Otherwise there's no dying for anybody,
no crisp rewards.

Batman came out and clubbed me.
He never did get along with my view of the universe.
except you know existential threads
from the time of the peace beaters and more.
He patted his dog Pastor Fido.
There was still so much to be learned
and even more to be researched.
It was like a goodbye. Why not accept it,
anyhow? The mission girls came through the woods
in their special suitings. It was all whipped cream and baklava.

Is there a Batman somewhere, who notices us
and promptly looks away, at a new catalog, say,
or another racing car expletive
coming back at Him?

In the airy, light-admitting, open-plan lyrics of John Ashbery's 2015 collection, *Breezeway*, there's a generous measure of sheer fun, and the title-poem is no exception. But the game-plan here seems to include playing hide and seek with retribution: there's the hurricane as well as the casual breeze, and God as well as the dog.

A breezeway is a corridor between buildings; one of its functions is to accommodate high winds. As a potential communal space in a hive of private ownership, its desirability would easily attract a neighbourhood dispute. The poem's soundscape catches fragments of argument, and commentary on the argument. Interruptions and misunderstandings are hinted: 'Someone said…', 'Alas it wasn't my call. / I didn't have a call…', 'It was like a goodbye'. It's striking how many short sentences and end-stopped lines there are. The supreme singer of *bel canto* seems a little angry, though his staccato dances on the feet of jokes.

Reviewing *Breezeway* in the *New Yorker*, Dan Chiasson hears mis-hearings in the poem: 'bark down' for 'back down' and 'break down', for instance. In Ashbery's lexicon, definitions proliferate like stem cells. 'Bark down', line 2, may connect, via comic antithesis, to 'bark up' as in 'to bark up the wrong tree'. If you bark something down, you probably shout it down, an interpretation that would fit the theory of the poem as variations on a quarrel. Imagine barked shins. Imagine a breezeway in which a dog barks maddeningly at nothing. Perhaps it's Pastor Fido, who has a small part in the next stanza. Meanwhile, 'jugularly' is a fine 4-syllable adverb, a choking mouthful of violence which suggests shoving down as well as shouting down. This breezeway might be the locus of social control.

The amused impatience of the poem swells into allegory, pushing beyond the parochial towards the chiliastic. It's like that cartoon-character of a breeze who, at the end of the first stanza, 'falls from a nearby tower / finds no breezeway, goes away / along a mission to supersize red shutters'. (Notice the odd directional hinge of 'away / along' and how well the unexpected preposition, 'along', amplifies the scope and physicality of the 'mission'.

Elias/Elijah was an Old Testament prophet, and he plays a related role in the poem. God, you'll recall, challenged Elijah by means of wind, earthquake and fire, though it turned out that he, God, wasn't in any of them: on this occasion, he was the 'still, small voice'. The possibly spiritual dimension of the 'call' in Breezeway is buffeted by phrases like 'dull-spirited winch', 'children's belongings', 'stuff like that'. The speaker's identification as a winch might be a reminder that poetry is not wholly a call (ing): it's heavy lifting-work – like getting agreement for a breezeway, like dying.

The delicious response to the question about 'children's belongings' seems to correct some unknown person's misapprehension: 'I said we were all homers not homos'. Either designation might explain an absence of kids. It's a brilliant throw-away remark, turning on that serendipitous near-homonym, and we smile, but perhaps uncomfortably. This is where the weight of the parochial is felt. Perhaps Hurricane Edsel is a windy homophobe. Why shouldn't a failed car turn into a caricature of machismo?

The stanza's last 3 lines stoically accept defeat and outline a moral imperative. Dying is the release to be earned when we (poets?) 'live out our precise experimentation'. There's not much time to mull this profundity over, or worry whether 'crisp rewards' is about cremation. In the next stanza, we shift to a new frame, and bathos strikes in the blunt past-historic: 'Batman came out and clubbed me'. Is 'Batman' Batman, or a nickname for some angry, verbally brutal dog-lover, kitted out by the poet's imagination as an evangelical form of the super-hero, his mutt a Christlike faithful shepherd? Perhaps he's related to those sugary 'mission girls… / in their special suitings', who arrive in the last stanza to deliver angelic calories.

Connections become increasingly tricky. Those 'Existential threads', for instance… are they remnants of the speaker's un-Batmanic 'view of the universe', related to string theory or even the threads on an Internet forum? 'Peace beaters' could denote drummers, dating from a period back in the 20th century when all kinds of activities, including sex, were believed to be capable of delivering world peace. My favourite lines deliver the aphorism, 'There was still so much to be learned / and even more to be researched', a wry motto for our academic times.

There may be wisdom in *not* researching Ashbery's meanings. Why not be Taoist about it and go with the flow, enjoying the surreal possibilities of the mental journey as Frank O'Hara enjoyed the changing imagery of the city streets? Well, yes, but Ashbery's poems insist on syntactical and moral logic. His caricatures are satirical in intent, and metaphysical hunger abides. That Batman-God who 'promptly looks away' the minute he notices one of his creatures raises the stakes. He will not reveal himself in any rushing wind. He won't be descending into the breezeway. The 'racing car expletive' (a cartoon car-noise?) seems to be bothering Him. When it comes to disputes with the neighbours, He may be as cagey as the poet – and the breeze.

https://www.theguardian.com/books/2015/jun/08/ poem-of-the-week-breezeway-by-john-ashbery

ELAINE FEINSTEIN

April Fools' Day

i.m. Isaac Rosenberg (1890–1918)

Does anybody know what it was all for?
Not Private Rosenberg, short as John Keats.
A nudge from Ezra Pound took him to war,
to sleep on boards, in France, with rotting feet,
writing his poetry by candle ends.
His fellow soldiers always found him odd.
Outsiders do not easily make friends
if they are awkward – with a foreign God.

He should have stayed in Cape Town with his sister.
Did he miss Marsh's breakfasts at Gray's Inn,
or Café Royal? He longed for the centre
though he was always shy with Oxbridge toffs –
he lacked the sexy eyes of Mark Gertler –
and his *Litvak* underlip could put them off.
'*From Stepney East!*' as Pound wrote
Harriet Monroe, while sending poems to her.

He died on April Fools' Day on patrol,
beyond the corpses lying in the mud,
carrying up the line a barbed wire roll
– useless against gunfire – with the blood
and flesh of Death in the spring air.
His was the life half lived, if even that,
and the remains of it were never found. We remember
the iron honey gold, his cosmopolitan rat.

Elaine Feinstein's collection, *Portraits*, is a gallery of tributes to a range of biographical figures. Not all are literary: there are singers and musicians (Edith Piaf, Louis Armstrong), and even a politician – Benjamin Disraeli. *Portraits* is a retrospective exhibition about the author, too, the summary of a long and varied writing-life narrated through the stories of the friends and inspirers who have accompanied her.

These figures, however admired, are not idealised, and neither is Isaac Rosenberg, the subject of 'April Fools' Day'. His treatment verges on the brusque. Yet by the end of the poem he is established as one of the artists with whom Feinstein most deeply sympathises.

Rosenberg died in the Great War on April 1st. 1918, at the Battle of Arras. Feinstein's title not only alludes to the day of Rosenberg's death: it implicates self-sacrifice, and perhaps war itself, in folly. 'Does anybody know what it was all for?' the speaker asks. 'Not Isaac Rosenberg.' Right away, he's the baffled anti-hero personified.

The poem runs swiftly through the basic facts. Feinstein has not published a biography of Rosenberg, as far as I know, but she draws on her biographer's skill for condensing the details and shaping the bigger picture. The narrative is loosely tethered by an ABABCDCD rhyme scheme, reversing linear chronology in the first two stanzas, so we begin with the war. The oddness of Rosenberg's behaviour and appearance is established early and forms a recurring motif. We're left in no doubt that the young artist was unattractive, socially inept – and short.

Rosenberg was 'short as John Keats' – a fact which had led to his relegation to a bantam regiment, where the slight stature of the conscripts often reflected childhood malnutrition. The mysterious 'nudge from Ezra Pound' was not the only pressure that sent him to war: family poverty was a consideration.(The 'mystery' was helpfully clarified in the subsequent discussion, by the poster Craxton, who quoted a draft of Rosenberg's 1915 letter to Pound. 'As to your suggestion about the Army, I think the world has been terribly damaged by certain poets (in fact any poet) in this stupid business. There is a certain temptation to join when you are making no money.'

Disclosure of his background (his family were Jewish Lithuanian émigrés) is postponed to the next stanza. It follows Pound's famous quip, snobby as well as anti-Semitic, when writing to Harriet Monroe about Rosenberg and recommending the young 'burglar's' poems for publication ('*Stepney East!*'). The title 'Private Rosenberg' reminds us he was not, and never rose, to the rank of Officer: he scribbled his last poems in the cesspit of the trenches. 'Rotting feet' and 'candle ends' sum it up. The last line of stanza one alludes, again obliquely, to anti-Semitism. Perhaps, though, that 'Foreign God' additionally represents poetry.

The second stanza returns the young conscript to happier times. But, again, a wrong direction is taken – the decision to leave Cape Town. The abrupt movement of the verse, casual diction and underplayed rhymes add to the sensation of a life crowded with event. Rosenberg was getting attention. He was a gifted painter, and had embarked on a not unexciting career. But it's clear that he was never the master of his fate. Even before life in the trenches, there was too little room for examining options, taking the longer perspective, making choices. He belonged, after all, to the un-leisured class.

In stanza 3 the scepticism of the opening question re-emerges in the remark about barbed wire being 'useless against gunfire'. The reference to 'the blood / and flesh of Death in the spring air' is a sudden, sharp lift-off to a rhetorical level which the poem has otherwise strenuously denied itself. Despite the matter-of-fact reference to the life half-lived, imagery from Rosenberg's poems, particularly 'August, 1914', shifts the tonal register from wry, pointed biography to the elegiac.

'Three lives hath one life- / Iron, honey, gold. / The gold, the honey gone – / Left is the hard and cold.' The three symbolic elements from Rosenberg's quatrain, fused together without punctuation, are transmuted into the richer substance, the life of poetry.

https://www.theguardian.com/books/booksblog/2015/mar/30/poem-of-the-week-april-fools-day-by-elaine-feinstein

MAYA CHOWDHRY

Microbial Museum

April ship sets sail, sea freezes ripples, leaves Rothera
behind. One hundred and fifty thousand years of snowfall in

cylindrical samples, bubble-wrapped, boxed in styrofoam,
cores wrenched from ice caverns to Immingham.

Drill incises annulus ice cuttings spiral surface. Statistics
held in water vapour measure up to eons of weather.

Blueprints of other lives, the oldest ice sequesters
reservoirs of extinct creatures resurrected.

Suspending cable sonars frozen microbial cells
immortal bugs from bacteriasicles emerge, grow, divide.

Prehistoric pestilence thaws, allows ancient genes to mix with
modern ones. Skiing genotype slaloms through DNA markers,

mutating the ocean, creeping into the unsuspecting cells
of species climbing the ladder to life.

The future is thawed, dispatched into a white out.

Martin Redfern's Polar Diary provides some useful background to this week's poem. 'Microbial Museum' begins with the 'April ship' departing from Rothera, Adelaide Island, where the BAS Research Station is based. Its cargo, thrillingly representing '(O)one hundred and fifty thousand years of snowfall' in the soil samples yielded by 'cores wrenched from ice caverns' is in transport to Immingham. At this point in the poem, guided by the title, readers might assume the samples are set to become an addition to an exhibition of ancient microbes. I looked up Immingham Museum to see if it housed such an exhibition. Not so far, it seems: you'd need to travel to Amsterdam to visit Artis Micropia.

Micropia sounds a fascinating place, featuring living microbes, virtual microbes and interactive installations like the 'Kiss O Meter' whose function you probably don't need anyone to explain. The museum's stated goal is to promote a positive view of microbes, provide 'an international platform for microbiology that brings diverse interest groups together in order to bridge the gap between science and the general public' and to encourage more study and research into 'micro-nature'. Maya Chowdhry would probably empathise with these aims. While she devotes her recent collection, *Fossil,* to investigating, with wit and precision, unusual geological phenomena and the life-cycles of various under-sung species, her larger goal is public and eco-political.

Chowdhry relishes scientific vocabulary, and naturalises it. The terse, compressed, 'notebook' syntax she favours in 'Microbial Museum' creates documentary immediacy, an impression of events happening in quick succession, and a vertically layered depth to the language. Connective words – main verbs, articles, etc. and punctuation details like the apostrophe 's' as used to indicate the possessive – may be excluded, while nouns compact into lists. They generate heat, like bodies working at some heavy physical task out of doors in sub-zero temperatures. By contrast, there's a developing ethereal quality to the lines in which 'Statistics / held in water vapour measure up to eons of weather'.

Chowdhry is more interested in thinking about what happens in the dark hiding places underground, or in a hypothetical future, than in Antarctic picture-painting. She's particularly aware of sound, making the ice-cores spark and hiss as the '(D)drill incises annulus ice cuttings spiral surface', or catching the potential rustle of wings and chitin in those 'reservoirs of extinct creatures resurrected'.

At the sixth couplet, a new and violent narrative emerges for the microbes. They are not simply to be disinterred and studied, but actually resurrected by the addition of new genetic material. The invasiveness of this process is expressed in the skiing metaphor of line 12.

The poem knows that the ethics of de-extinction are dubious. Does our species' uncontrollable inventiveness mitigate its ecological impudence, can we fix the disruption human advancement causes by an even more advanced kind of human advancement? Perhaps, if all else fails, we can abandon earth and colonise Mars. Did I say 'we'? Well, perhaps not everyone will be on that space-ship. And how do we know we will always be clever enough and quick enough for real damage limitation?

As it develops, this poem's focus by-passes the melting glaciers and other 'usual suspects' which, tragically, have almost become clichés of global warming. In a collection which mostly delights in biodiversity, the apocalypse suddenly appears, and the bacteria of some 'prehistoric pestilence' return to the ecosystem through a horrible collision of 'ancient genes' and 'modern ones'. 'Skiing genotype slaloms through DNA markers, // mutating the ocean, creeping into the unsuspecting cells / of species climbing the ladder to life.' The final image recalls Antarctic weather conditions while bringing back the danger-verb, 'thaw', in a compelling oxymoron: 'The future is thawed, dispatched into a white out.'

Chowdhry is an adventurous transmedia writer, artist and collaborator. Her work is no less alive on the page, and *Fossil* reveals one of the most appealing voices of the evolving eco-poetry continent, connecting to the magic and multiplicity of the biosphere while honouring fact, and sounding warnings. Her poems discover 'thoughts that do often lie too deep for in tears', not only in wild flowers, but in fossil butterflies, lava, carrots and Black Badger Carlin Peas. And they know that tears are not all that's needed: what's needed now are images and thoughts which lead to action.

https://www.theguardian.com/books/booksblog/2017/dec/11/poem-of-the-week-microbial-museum-by-maya-chowdhry

R.F. LANGLEY

To a Nightingale

Nothing along the road. But
petals, maybe. Pink behind
and white inside. Nothing but
the coping of a bridge. Mutes
on the bricks, hard as putty,
then, in the sun, as metal.
Burls of *Grimmia,* hairy,
hoary, with their seed-capsules
uncurling. Red mites bowling
about on the baked lichen
and what look like casual
landings,striped flies, *Helina,*
Phaonia, could they be?
This month the lemon, I'll say
primrose-coloured, moths, which flinch
along the hedge then turn in
to hide, are Yellow Shells not
Shaded Broad-bars. Lines waver.
Camptogramma. Heat off the
road and the nick-nack of names.
Scotopteryx. Darkwing. The
flutter. Doubles and blurs the
margin. Fuscous and white. Stop
at nothing. To stop here at
nothing, as a chaffinch sings
interminably, all day.
A chiff-chaff. Purring of two
turtle doves. Voices, and some
vibrate with tenderness. I
say none of this for love. It

is anyone's giff-gaff. It
is anyone's quelque chose.
No business of mine. Mites which
ramble. Caterpillars which
curl up as question marks. Then
one note, five times, louder each
time, followed, after a fraught
pause, by a soft cuckle of
wet pebbles, which I could call
a glottal rattle. I am
empty, stopped at nothing, as
I wait for this song to shoot.
The road is rising as it
passes the apple tree and
makes its approach to the bridge.

Less than 200 pages long, R.F. Langley's *Complete Poems* is a nightingale- rather than an ostrich-sized body of work, but, as its editor Jeremy Noel-Tod observes, few collections can rival the 'intensity of perception and perfection of finish'.

Among the most readable of the avant-garde poets, Langley has occasionally stirred in me what I term the Kenneth Williams effect. The wonderful fabric of his observation would suddenly break or knot, at which point I'd think, 'Oh, stop messin' about. You're too good for trendy-bendy tricks'.

But I was wrong. These weren't tricks but simply flying sparks, thrown off by language during the process of cutting and drilling through to a cleaner kind of origination. Certainly in the post-millennial collections, there's no sense of participation in any langpo-regiment's smart-bombing of the synapses. Langley is a purer breed of iconoclast, on a scrupulous quest for revealing what his eye has seen and his mind understood. Despite some serious play, he doesn't mess about.

'To a Nightingale', the final poem in the volume, reveals the extent and delicacy of his iconoclasm. ny reader lured by the title to expect either a Keatsian nightingale or a parody of that species, will be disappointed. Langley presents a meticulously observed ornithological portrait. But, like the good naturalist and narrator he is, he defers the encounter, inviting us to first explore the Suffolk scene and notice its flora and fauna. Insects feature in some detail: if the nightingale addressed in the title could read English poetry, she would no doubt appreciate the detour around her chosen diet.

Etymology and entomology seem closely affiliated as the poem's eye flickers between descriptive methods. The image-making, for all its vivid quickness, seems to involve as precise selection as the taxonomy: 'Red mites bowling / about on the baked lichen…' In addition, the codes of a particular landscape are offered for our deciphering: the dried 'mutes' on the brickwork, for instance, signify the presence of raptors, but probably not very recently: the particular kind of moss, Grimmia, means conditions are usually moist. Thought processes themselves may be exposed. The note-maker hesitates to identify the striped flies he sees and leaves the question of identification casually open '*Helina, / Phaonia*, could they be?' Like a scrupulous water-colourist, he hesitates over the exact shade of the yellow moths' perhaps fluctuating colouration: 'This month the lemon, I'll say / primrose-coloured, moths, which flinch / along the hedge then turn in / to hide, are Yellow Shells not / Shaded Broad-bars.' Langley's linguistic precision-engineering requires terms like *camptogramma* and *scotoperyx* but no less important is the recorded movement of his own perception. The greatest miracle in these lines, though, lies in the combination of verbs and appositions: 'flinch / along…', 'turn it / to hide'.

Strolling on, the speaker begins fine-tuning his bird-recording equipment. The mimesis is delicate and complex. Earlier, although the insects were vividly imagined, the poem itself resisted any insect-imitating devices. Now, even the stop-start, notebook-jotting movement of the syntax and lineation seems birdlike. Avian and human activity seem to meet as tenor and vehicle might in a seamless metaphor. Perhaps Keats isn't quite so far away?

The various, ever-fluttering moths and the chaffinch, who continuously sings, exemplify creatures which stop 'at nothing' – a significant and ambiguous phrase, to be repeated later, combining two nearly opposite meanings. For the far-from-reckless human in the picture, stopping at nothing implies stasis rather than headlong rush. His art of seeing is like the art of dying: it's to stop gracefully at the point where 'nothing' is all that's visible.

'Voices, and some / vibrate with tenderness' follows the note about the two 'purring' turtle doves. Then it's as if the poet reins himself back. 'I / say none of this for love.' The diction has been so alive and alert with feeling that the sudden assertion forms a nothing that stops the reader. 'I say' doesn't mean 'I believe', of course, and the throw-away-learned phrase 'anyone's giff-gaff', nicely minting a rhyme for chiff-chaff, makes extra mischief with its double-meaning – 'mutual giving' in Scots but also a modern telecommunications network, Giffgaff. What's rejected is the vagueness of a word like 'love' and the deforming romanticism of self-projection onto other species: 'No business of mine.'

And, thus unprepared, we suddenly almost get to meet the nightingale. There is a beautiful passage later ('soft cuckle of / wet pebbles') but the sound-recordist wants us to know about the repetition and the 'glottle rattle'. As for the daylight performance of the famous song, it's anticipated rather than activated. 'I wait / for this song to shoot', says the poet having reminded us that emptiness is the precondition for hearing. In any case, the poem doesn't need to tell the nightingale. The listener takes his leave of us with an amused flourish, a scattering of affirmative symbols: 'The road is rising as it / passes the apple tree and / makes its approach to the bridge.' Instead of the song itself, we have the shift of perspective, the new long view, opening out and offered generously at the point where we might least expect it: at the end of the poem, at the end of a life's work, at the end of a life.

https://www.theguardian.com/books/booksblog/2016/may/16/poem-of-the-week-to-a-nightingale-by-rf-langley

JEAN 'BINTA' BREEZE

Tweet Tweet

There's a blackbird
in my mango tree
and I think of Marley
and singing songs of freedom

I have followed birds
from hills
to home
and back
and wondering where was Zion

but now I am content
on this verandah

the blackbirds come to my mango tree
and sing

home is always
where it's meant to be

I'm sure
that's what blackbirds sing

'Tweet Tweet', from Jean 'Binta' Breeze's latest Bloodaxe collection, *The Verandah Poems,* twins the sense-delighting symbols of hope and home, the mango-tree and the blackbird. Even the just-possible allusion to Twitter is benign in the context: those 280-character tweets don't always divide and disturb us, after all. They can reconnect scattered homes and form new ones across continents.

The symbolism of bird and tree is heightened in the culminating lines of the opening stanza, where the speaker 'think(s) of Marley / and singing songs of freedom...' Listening to Breeze, who's often described as the first woman Dub poet, I was surprised and delighted to hear her on youtube singing part of the same 'Redemption Song'. She is a magnificent performer and in this earlier recording of her work there's a powerful and overt political thrust. So in 'Tweet Tweet' the blackbird and the mango tree transcend stereotypes, signifying 'freedom songs'.

The poem's redemption story is simpler than the one Marley tells, and relies more on an audience to provide context. Yet its hesitations and questions reflect something of Marley's haunted lyricism: 'I have followed birds / from hills / to home / and back / and wondering where was Zion'. 'Tweet Tweet' has a fragmented melody that pleases the ear, and, at the same time, an appearance that satisfies the eye. I like the way the text occupies the page, as if allowing light to penetrate through the short, spare lines and frequent stanza-breaks.

Characteristically, Breeze's poems are more than personal: they gather up and speak for a collective experience, often the experience of women. Here, the big, sacred, Rastafari vision of Zion, and associated political triumph, contrasts with the smaller, domestic concept of home, almost as traditionally masculine and feminine values might contend with each other. In 'wondering where was Zion' the poet hints at irony, and the reader might also notice, embedded in the sound of the cleverly chosen present-participle, 'wondering', the 'wandering' of a traveller between unsatisfied versions of home. This second stanza evokes restlessness, despite the stops it makes to draw a strong breath at the line-breaks. An ancient weariness pervades the movement 'from hills / to home / and back'. Blackbirds fly more easily to their chosen tree, their mango-Zion.

There are probably at least fourteen ways of looking at the blackbird (s) in this poem. Taking the ornithological option first, I found out that the Jamaican Blackbird is a 'highly adaptive bird,' a forest-dweller with a 'wheezing call'. So perhaps it's not the one in the poem. If Breeze's blackbird belongs to the more widespread 'common' species (which sometimes migrates), it could be seen as the unifying factor in the poet's interpretation of 'home'. Breeze, I understand, has bases in the Caribbean and in England: she may well be 'at home' with the 'English' blackbirds' song. Transplanted to the mango-tree, that song may complicate ideas of home.

The blackbirds' message, 'home is always / where it's meant to be' seems, however, to be unambiguous. There's a faintly religious intonation: things which are 'meant to be' are thought traditionally to be divinely decreed, or at least ordained by fate. The recovery of home, post-diaspora, might be seen as guaranteed by birth-right. The embedded pun in 'blackbirds' is light-touch, sure-footed, and it grounds the poem. There's an echo in the last two lines, perhaps, of Paul Lawrence Dunbar and Maya Angelou ('I know why the caged bird sings') But here the cage is open, and the bird still sings.

Despite the glow of celebration and the touch of irony (not forgetting that of the title), Tweet Tweet is a strong-minded poem of identity, contentedly asserting its principles and priorities. Home is never simply a place: it's a construct of imagination. For the poet, it's earthed in a very specific location where she sits writing, recuperating, socialising – her Jamaican verandah during the long, warm months of the mango-season.

https://www.theguardian.com/books/booksblog/2017/apr/03/poem-of-the-week-tweet-tweet-by-jean-binta-breeze

TONY CONRAN

Jasper

for John Jones the potter

Waxwork of a crag, a model of sea rock
In gleaming maroon –
Hear the waves break on it, see the fish fly
Under the moon!

A piece of witch-stone, jasper,
Red chalcedony
With a tidewash of grey quartz still ebbing
Back like the sea.

I was given it, it has lain in my hearth
Nearly a year
To give peace by arbitrary charm
To fingerers here.

Each hand that stroked it, gave to and took
Power out of it:
Love warmed it with whitsun, it knew
Fire-tonguing wit.

It felt stillness in half-light, it learned
Like a wild foal
To stand calm in a crowdful of noise
In its deep quartz soul.

It is Welsh rock, John. A vein of it runs
In the nape
Of the hanging coast where the oaktrees
Knot the Straits into shape.

Earth, water and fire! and a girl's hand that gave it
Dearer to me
Than gold! – I send you this shard from the wheel
Of the Welsh sea.

Your potter's eyes found glazes in red grit –
You made them yours,
The piebald debris of metallic earths,
Ragbag of ores.

We finger a pebble for luck, or chance
Magic try –
But your fingers have lived with luck so long
They must have it, or die.

And your hands chance no amateur magic:
The wheel must turn,
The wet grey clay must rise like a genie
To teapot or urn.

Yet now, because you have left Wales, and sold
Kiln and wheel
And because your cottage sinks down to its knees
In an overgrown field,

And the racks in your front room shop
No longer fill
Quietly, quietly with the cups and jugs
Of your fingers' skill

And because now, though the potter's gone
And the clay dries dead,
We are glad that the love of a bride
Has graced your bed –

That ancient, amateur magic of hands,
A love and a luck
Richer than even from clay
Ever was struck –

Because of all this, on your wedding day
I send
All the power in a stone I can
To make and mend:

A piece of witch-stone, jasper,
Red chalcedony
With a tidewash of grey quartz still ebbing
Back to the sea.

'Jasper' by the Welsh poet, critic and translator, Tony Conran (1931–2013) is from his 1998 collection, *Eros Proposes a Toast: Collected Public Poems and Gifts*, and testifies to a further talent, that of friendship. The book celebrates 'the heart's affections' and that heart's larger community. It's unusual to read a collection in English of poems in which other lives are so integral to the text and the texture of feeling. But in Wales the idea of a sociable poetry does not run counter to the cultural grain. Conran's occasion-celebrating poems, which may include fragments of the dedicatees' life-story and glimmers of their personality, draw the reader, too, into the circle.

This poem's occasion is the marriage of 'John Jones the potter'. Jones has already left Wales, and so melancholy is folded into celebration. The gift of jasper from the poet's own hearth is special, indeed sacred, because the speaker views it as witness and participant in human connective ritual: 'Love warmed it with whitsun, it knew / Fire-tonguing wit.' The lower-case 'w' of 'whitsun' alerts us to a personal calendar. not only the prerogative of the church, and the nice abbreviation of 'fire-tonguing wit' gives a human face to Pentecost.

In the *llatai* ('messenger') genre of Welsh poetry, the speaker despatches a creature or object to bear his words of desire to the beloved. Conran's 'message' is for an absent friend, not a lover, but the tone is nonetheless impassioned. Personal celebration is interwoven with emotive ideas about art and nationhood.

Importantly, John Jones is a fellow-artist. The poem makes no distinction between art and craft: as the narrative evolves, it becomes clear that the same rules, the same unpredictable 'magic', operate for craftsman and wordsmith alike. The potter deftly uses the wheel that defines him as a professional: Conran, in Bardic tradition, has the discipline of rhymed, stanzaic form. The potter's eye is close to the ground, where he discovers his materials and ideas: 'glazes in red grit' and '(T)he piebald debris of metallic earths, / Ragbag of ores'. Similarly, the poet's diction is about tangibility, texture, location.

The poem begins with the jasper in vigorous, descriptive close-up. There are encircling mages of the actual and symbolic: 'Waxwork of a crag, a model of sea rock / In gleaming maroon…' Continuous, small, renewing surges of narrative energy, the stanzas rise and break like a series of waves. In the alternating long/short lineation, there's a tidal sense of coming and going, giving and taking, gaining and losing, ending and beginning. The potter's wheel is identified with the sea in stanza 4. The poem, too, is a wheel and a sea.

A direct appeal to the reader-recipient's historical and poetic imagination enlarges the territory: 'Hear the waves break on it, see the fish fly / Under the moon!' And then comes the climax and the direct address of stanza 6: 'It is Welsh rock, John', followed by the revelation in stanza 7 that it was originally a prized gift, from a loved girl, *to* the poet.

Magic connects to love in the story of the stone. It's first sounded in the 'witch-stone' of stanza 2 and taken up in the 'genie' comparison in 10. Significantly, this is 'arbitrary charm' and 'chance magic'. The word 'amateur' (originally meaning 'lover of') heralds the more overt presence of of Eros among the makers, and stanza 13's compensatory gladness that, in the marriage bed, another kind of magic, 'ancient and amateur', will be set in motion. Although 'bed' is rhymed with 'dead', the moment of imagined sterility is soon absorbed. Hands will act again to make something greater than 'teapot or urn': to make love and life itself. The poet-speaker doesn't set art above Eros. Eros wins the day.

A specific North Wales landscape is evoked 'where the oaktrees / '(K)knot the Straits into shape' and the abandoned cottage 'sinks down to its knees / In an overgrown field'. That last image turns the poem towards departure and decline: 'And the racks in your front room shop / No longer fill / Quietly, quietly with he cups and jugs / Of your fingers' skill...' Boarded shops lining a high street, a village's single village-shop with its fading 'Am Werth' (For Sale) sign – both sadly familiar views are evoked by the potter's emigration.

Sometimes, what might be a Welsh-language-inspired verbal pattern adds an extra volt of rhythmic electricity (e.g. the inversion in 'We finger a pebble for luck, or chance / Magic try' or the complex interchange in the first two lines of stanza 4). The poem functions by both accumulation and repetition, its tactile quality emphasised by hands and 'fingerers'.

But, while the Welshness of the jasper 'crag' is emphasised, and the small piece of rock is almost Wales in miniature, the poem is culturally connected and contains possibilities for broader readings. You might be reminded of the potter's-shop stanzas in Fitzgerald's translation, 'The Rubaiyat of Omar Khayyam', or the ekphrastic passages in Keats's 'Ode on a Grecian Urn'. Classical, Islamic and pre-Christian Celtic 'worlds' press close together, without conflict, honouring the stone's hoped-for power 'to make and mend'.

https://www.theguardian.com/books/booksblog/2016/apr/25/poem-of-the-week-jasper-by-tony-conran

SAUNDERS LEWIS
Lavernock

translated by Harry Gilonis

Moor and sea, skylark's song
ascending through the wind's demesnes,
we too standing listening
as we'd listened formerly.

What wealth remains, then, after
the journey's adversities?
Moor and sea, skylark's song
descending from the wind's demesnes.

Lavernock

Gwaun y môr, cân ehedydd
yn esgyn drwy libart y gwynt,
ninnau'n sefyll i wrando
fel y gwrandawem gynt.

Be' sy'n aros, pa gyfoeth,
wedi helbulon ein hynt?
Gwaun y môr, cân ehedydd
yn disgyn o libart y gwynt.

The music of 'Lavernock' begins, in both languages, with the same word, the place-name of the title. Harry Gilonis's translation of this brief lyric by the writer, politician and Welsh-language activist Saunders Lewis (1893–1950) goes on to quietly re-sound, in stately tetrameter rhythms, the assonance of the original – and to capture the essence of its 'timeless' images.

'Lavernock' is also a reminder, as each new year is a reminder, of the psychological resonance humans find in the seasonal cycle. Its narrative is shaped by the arc of return. The first stanza, impressionistically structured, reveals that the speaker and companion have come back to a place they have visited, perhaps more than once, in a previous period of their lives: 'standing listening / as we'd listened formerly'. Repetition of the experience suggests they might potentially be able to share the landscape's seeming timelessness.

The adverb of the fourth line is a pun in English, and that differently spelled word, *formally*, quietly nuances the reading of *formerly*. It may subliminally enable us to register the decorum of tone, the restraint of any self-indulgent nostalgia.

Another shape in the flow-chart of the poem is the ascent and descent of the skylark's song, mirroring the movement of the bird. A slightly slower-moving and longer line records the ascent of the lark as it rises gradually higher and higher in the first stanza: there's a quicker pulse and, sometimes, a gentle tumbling movement in the second.

Gilonis's choice of vocabulary interlaces the richly abstract and the sparely descriptive. The freight carried by words such as 'demesnes', 'adversities' and even 'wealth' is social as well as linguistic. Their plenitude implies limitation, in contrast with the plain monosyllables, 'wind', 'moor' and 'sky', which proclaim the expansive and archetypal.

A sentimental reader might expect the sentimental answer to the question, 'What wealth remains, then, after / the journey's adversities?'. The unexpected answer, returning us to the two opening lines, refutes the easy gesture ('our love remains, naturally!') and recharges the crux of the question, the meaning of 'wealth'.

The descent to earth of the larksong occurs without drama, indeed with inevitability. Chiasmus creates an impression of seclusion and safety, an assumption that Lavernock remains, and will remain, with or without human witness. The continuity of the moor, the skylark's song, the wind and the sea is unquestioned. To this extent, Lewis's vision is Romantic.

A later generation, ours, is not so certain, and evocations of natural beauty may remind us of equally 'natural' human predation and cast a shadow over the poem. As we attune to the close listening and tactility of this poem and its translation we're reminded that such qualities are integral to the well-examined life.

The first wireless signal, transmitted from Lavernock Point in Morse code by Marconi and his assistant, included the words, *Can you hear me?* The art of listening is taught also by the questions – and the mysterious music – heard in these two poems.

I am grateful to the copyright-holder, Siwan Jones, for permission to feature Lavernock, and to the University of Wales Press for putting me in touch with her.

https://www.theguardian.com/books/booksblog/2018/dec/31/poem-of-the-week-lavernock-by-saunders-lewis

MIRIAM NASH

The Walking Father Blues

How does a father leave his life?
Easy, a pair of walking shoes
And who can hear them but his wife
walking the walking father blues?

Easy, the pair of walking shoes
lead him at last to his new door
walking the walking father blues
for the new wife says she'll wait no more

Lead him at last to his new door!
The door knob does not strike him down
and the new wife says she'll wait no more
wrapped in the old one's dressing-gown

The door knob does not strike him down
the clock must race to meet their time
Wrapped in the old one's dressing-gown
the new wife says they've done no crime

The clock must race to meet their time
the mugs swing neatly from their hooks
the new wife says they've done no crime
and dances while the father cooks

The mugs swing neatly from their hooks
she locks the windows, bars the gate
she dances while the father cooks
for her body holds a lovely weight

She locks the windows, bars the gate
she hides his battered walking shoes
and holds her body's lovely weight
for she will not sing her child the blues

She hides the battered walking shoes
for who must fear them but a wife
who will not sing her child the blues
of how a father leaves his life.

'The Walking Father Blues' comes from a strong and varied first collection, *All the Prayers in the House,* by the young Scottish poet, Miriam Nash. Like her mentor Mimi Khalvati, Nash excels at both 'free' and 'formal' verse. When well-executed, this kind of mixing in a collection sharpens the outlines of each poem, without suggesting a war of words, 'poetries' or selves. The flexible approach aids narrative diversity: this is important for Nash, because, as well as drawing on intertextual sources (Orcadian Selkie legend, the works of Robert Louis Stevenson, etc,) she has many family-stories to tell – quirky, complex, tragic, comic and often all these things simultaneously.

If you're interested in poetic form, you'll know the pantoum, or pantun, has an intriguing colonial history. The first English translation was included by William Marsden in the Malayan Grammar he published with OUP in 1812. Later on, the pantoum was transported to France by Ernest Fouinet, popularised by Victor Hugo, and explored by Baudelaire and others. It was originally an oral form, the quatrains rhyming abab, the lines, longer than in most English transplantations, composed of paired, two-to-three feet hemistichs. Second and fourth lines of each stanza become first and third lines of the next. In the last quatrain the first line of the poem becomes the last, and the third line, the second. Easy peasy? Yes and no.

'The Walking Father Blues', the first pantoum on 'Poem of the Week', is gently innovative. Take my word for it, Nash has consummate formal skills at her disposal. In grammatically tweaking her repeated lines and minimising punctuation she draws the pantoum back to its apparently more flexible Malayan roots. Her method helps the repetitions to sound inevitable and idiomatic, but, above all, it enhances narrative capacity. This is a poem with a big 'contemporary' theme, the break-up of one marriage, the formation of a new: it plays the freedom-grab against domestic consolidation, building stanzas like little fortresses around the relentless pace of 'the walking father'.

A strong, emotive subject also helps to push the pattern deeper into the reader's subconscious. One of the essential and most difficult arts of formal verse is to avoid producing an exoskeleton, a Natural History Museum exhibit where the bones are too brightly lit. In analysing the poem, it's interesting to look at the structure, of course, but important to keep sight of all that makes a viable organism – like those little rhythmic muscle-twitches cunningly eluding prosody's martial law (in this case, the iambic tetrameter).

Nash's poem counterpoints defiant optimism and fearful caution, guilt and innocence. The father walks. 'The door knob does not strike him down.' But no-one leaves without the possibility of the past catching up; the pantoum is a great vehicle for the narrative of the past catching up, a very configuration of a battle of the present to succeed the past. The new wife is 'wrapped in the old one's dressing gown' and, in a verbal shift to defending the new relationship, 'says they've done no crime'. She is actively strategic: she locks and bars the escape routes, hides the shoes. Because of the hard emotional knots, the lightness and magic of the attained new balance shines out: 'she dances while the father cooks'. Not until stanza 6 is the plot deepened with that most crucial piece of information: the new wife is pregnant. The narrator, reliably, we hope, asserts that the new wife and mother 'will not sing her child the blues / of how a father leaves his life'. The 'blues' is a past grief and a potential one, perhaps. As a form, blues doesn't shape the poem: as a mood, it resides with the abandoned first wife in stanza one, and doesn't hinder progress. Even when it's finished, the poem seems to be walking on.

https://www.theguardian.com/books/booksblog/2017/jul/03/ poem-of-the-week-the-walking-father-blues-by-miriam-nash

NAUSHEEN EUSUF

Poem for Professor Frye

> *'the pale dawn of longing', 'the broken collar-bone of silence', 'the massive eyelids of time', 'the crimson tree of love'. I have made these up myself, and they are free to any poet who wants them [...]*
> — *Northrop Frye,* Anatomy of Criticism

The pale dawn of longing descends,
ruthless and punctual in its disdain.
The soul, benumbed, dares not to face
the world outside the window frame,
and grips the bedclothes tight and close.

Father Time, with his massive eyelids
and crooked nose, has little time
for such inconsequence. He notes
the curled-up form and balled-up sheets,
and scorns the timorous race of men.

The silence glows like a broken bone
in an X-ray, where the flesh is dark,
and darker still the ghostly heart
that waters the crimson tree of love.

Northrop Frye wrote in *The Anatomy of Criticism* that 'poetry can only be made out of other poems; novels out of other novels... the forms of literature can no more exist outside literature than the forms of the sonata and fugue and rondo can exist outside music'. Whether you strongly agree with this, slightly agree, slightly disagree or stamp your foot in outrage, there's no denying that intertextuality, under less formal names (influence, conversation, etc.) has always been with us, and that it often liberates the inventive prowess of young poets.

Nausheen Eusuf enjoys some lively conversation, sometimes subversive, sometimes admiring, with other writers and texts in her first collection, *Not Elegy, but Eros.* She shouldn't be typecast by this predilection: Eusuf occupies wider worlds of public and personal engagement. But, then, her more 'literary' poems are never simply literary. This week's poem is a good example of how the intertextual chrysalis can open bright, original wings.

Frye's sardonic offer of those heavy-handed metaphors 'free to any poet who wants them' are from the Fourth Essay in the '*Anatomy*', 'Rhetorical Criticism: theory of genres'. Frye describes the general principle, and enthuses about the 'sudden glory of the fused metaphor' as the 'emotional crux of the lyric', citing classic examples, and subtler manifestations: Thomas Nashe's 'Brightness falls from the air' and Dylan Thomas's 'A grief ago'.

Pathetic fallacy of the obvious kind ('the pale dawn of longing') gets a new turn from Eusuf right away with the un-dawn-like verb, 'descends'. Her further characterisation of the dawn as 'ruthless and punctual in its disdain' leaves us in no doubt: the literary trope of the pale, pining lover is being translated into a convincing portrayal of depression. At the same time, a parodic nuance is suggested not only by the diction but the mixture of little stumbles (line 1) and careful precision (line 3) in the iambic tetrameter.

Although no persona or character has been defined, Eusuf's narrative picks up the note of self-dramatisation, and intensifies it with archaism, e.g. 'the soul, benumbed'. The expression hovers nearer pastiche as the second stanza progresses, and yet the idea of a soul physically able 'to grip the bedclothes tight and close' is oddly effective. If we forget the title, we could read this sort-of-a sonnet as every well-read non-poet's misery poem. It gestures ineptly at the romantic and metaphysical set texts. And yet the misery is never in doubt.

A central characteristic of this kind of poem is that it ignores the warning-signals an experienced writer would dodge from miles away. So Frye's personification of time leads Eusuf to present Father Time, that most stereotypical of allegorical figures. Only now he is transformed through caricature, the 'massive eyelids' complemented by the 'crooked nose' in a striking sketch of the Titan as old bruiser.

Father Time, it's comically noticed, has 'little time' for the protagonist's suffering. In fact, he 'scorns the timorous race of men'. This sounds like a quotation from some lofty minor Victorian, but, if it is, I couldn't locate it. It offers a revised characterisation, a Time living up to his weighty reputation (despite the broken nose).

The protagonist remains undefined, but details are suggestive. A foetal position is suggested by 'the curled-up form', the 'balled-up sheets' evoke anguished insomnia. But the form is not necessarily bodily: it could be the kind of impenetrable questionnaire you fill in and give up on. Those sheets could be abandoned poems or letters. Perhaps the 'longing' of the first line was directed not at a lost love, but worldlier hopes of achievement? The poem's emotions are masked; the voice and figures belong to a pre-confessional age.

It's the last stanza which gets to the crux of things. 'The silence glows like a broken bone' is a brilliant piece of synaesthesia, transforming Frye's comically precise non sequitur, 'the broken collar-bone of silence'. Eusuf's electric silence dramatises the extent of the loss. From the lit bone of the X-ray we penetrate darkness and further darkness. Love and the heart are old and jaded companions. But Eusuf's image is more anatomical, the veins and arteries of the lover's body forming the tree which is watered by the pumped out blood. It's an image which displays the intrinsic, physical nature of emotion.

The poem which began with Frye's array of deliberately inept and poet-patronising metaphors has found a pulse in them. To re-read it is to realise that Eusuf has outclassed Frye with a real love poem, literary in diction but not bowed by its borrowings, serious enough after all to be taken seriously. The poet has shown the critic that art can break the rules, and still shine.

https://www.theguardian.com/books/booksblog/2018/jun/18/ poem-of-the-week-poem-for-professor-frye-by-nausheen-eusuf

MILES BURROWS

But Those Unheard

The next poem we can't actually see.
In fact it may not be there at all.
But if it was there it would solve several problems
In the poems that we can see. We infer its existence
From what we believe to be its effects.
It may be a completely new kind of poem
Or something similar, that has leverage
On existing poems, being itself unreadable
And extremely heavy and moving at a high speed.
Heavy invisible rapid poem-like entities
Which may never be seen or felt, almost certainly underlie
Existing poems, and may outweigh them
As the dead outnumber the living.
And they have an activity, as the dead
Can bend existing poems and hold them together.
But these are not dead poems
(We haven't got a name for them yet).
They may explain shivering, wrinkles or otherwise unexplained anomalies
In poems we thought we understood. Lacunas,
Leanings, hesitations, small lapses in grammar, odd coinings,
Unexplained dashes or ashes where commas might be expected,
A wandering semicolon. Misspellings we pretended to ignore.
Two instances of *hapax legomena* in seventeeth century Siamese poems
Could be explained by a heavy unwritten poem-like entity (about the size of Denmark)
Passing rapidly very close to them or through them.
In fact the whole field of textual criticism
Has become much more exciting
As we study here underground in darkness and close to absolute silence
Poems we thought we remembered.

Miles Burrows's *Waiting for the Nightingale* is a charming and unusual volume of poems, elegantly constructed, largely rhyme-free but wildly funny. Burrows's subject is often, ostensibly, himself, his procedure to raise self-ridicule to an art-form. His specialism is the bizarrely real, rather than the surreal, inlaid with an affectionate but sharp social observation. Schooldays and the sexual comedy are often mined (in both senses of the verb), while, as you might guess from the Keatsian titles of both the collection and this week's poem, the art of poetry itself comes in for some tickling and teasing.

The poems in 'But Those Unheard' are mysterious phenomena. Burrows writes about them as if reporting a new planet or particle in the language of science as usually dispensed by the experts to the marvelling, maths-less masses. He has particular fun with the speculative aspects of science research and language (the 'wild surmise', as Keats might have said). Negatives rule: the not-heard, not-seen, possibly not-there-at-all are heavily present.

In carrying the hypothesising idiom over into a field where it's not usually found, or, at least, not so directly revealed, Burrows surprises us into amusement. But, alongside the de-familiarisation, a literary theory or two may also be glimpsed. The voice is not so single-mindedly satirical as to advertise that theory, in either discipline, is fake or absurd. In a way, there's a pact being secured. To understand the poetry cosmos, we need projections and models. We may 'see' the invisible, and postulate the unlikely in the search for a good reading.

The influential structures in 'But Those Unheard' are 'heavy, invisible rapid poem-like entities'. They may be the archetypal structures of a literary universe. They may be all the poems of the past, somehow pressing in on the present, altering it, and becoming, themselves, newly mysterious as they do so… 'But these are not dead poems / (We haven't got a name for them yet).' We might imagine them as Platonic Forms. The philosopher

Tim Ruggiero writes, 'The heart of the theory of Platonic forms is that they are true and beautiful and unchanging.' This leads naturally to Keats, of course, our hovering *genius loci* as he praises the eternal, and eternally inaudible, 'happy melodist' depicted on the Grecian Urn. Burrows's mock-lecture might be saying, wisely, that the concept of the poem can become too rigid and heavy for what happens where poetry is made. The poet's own concept may become restrictive. Burrows doesn't seem to be making obvious judgements about stereotypes, but when he jokes that 'It may be a completely new kind of poem' he definitely captures the imagination.

Individual words as well as poems are determined by these shadowy but increasingly tangible forces: so the cause of the occurrence of the 'two instances of *hapax legomena* in seventeenth century Siamese poems' is 'a heavy unwritten poem-like entity (about the size of Denmark) / Passing rapidly very close to them or through them'. *Hapax legomena* are words occurring only once in a given context. The poem's transformation of the speculative to the highly specific is not only funny and bizarre: it suggests that scholarly hubris is the target.

There are moments when it seems that neither poetry, cosmology or philosophy is the fundamental topic, and that, as for Keats in the Odes, the 'heavy unwritten' entity is death. One moment is in line 21, where 'dashes' mutates to 'ashes'. The parataxis of the preceding lines also has a disturbing effect: many of the words ('shivering', 'wrinkles', 'lacunas', 'hesitations'), although placed in fluent succession, actually represent interruptions of succession. In the list beginning with 'Lacunas' and ending with the 'wandering semicolon' a 'lapse' in formal grammar might be said to occur.

Clear intimations of mortality haunt the final two lines: 'As we study here underground in darkness and close to absolute silence / Poems we thought we remembered.' Darkness and silence may bring to mind the fruitful creative practice of the Celtic bards, but there's a more ominous connotation of mental darkness, and the frustrating if interesting struggle when we try to piece together lines once known by heart. It might be that these lost poems form the tenor of the poem's guiding cosmological metaphor. They are the mysterious 'poem-like entities' still present somewhere in our mental universe, still making brain-waves. The joke is that the very forgetfulness becomes a form of 'textual criticism' – and, of course, a reminder that critics can build whole theories on the basis of small comprehension, or none at all.

https://www.theguardian.com/books/booksblog/2017/jun/19/ poem-of-the-week-but-those-unheard-by-miles-burrows

KAMELA DAS

Someone Else's Song

I am a million, million people
Talking all at once, with voices
Raised in clamour, like maids
At village-wells.

I am a million, million deaths
Pox-clustered, each a drying seed
Someday to be shed, to grow for
Someone else, a memory.

I am a million, million births
Flushed with triumphant blood, each a growing
Thing that thrusts its long-nailed hands
To scar the hollow air.

I am a million, million silences
Strung like crystal beads
Onto someone else's
Song.

From Kamala Das's first poetry collection, *Summer in Calcutta* (1965), 'Someone Else's Song' is included in the generous selection of her work edited by Devindra Kohli for the Penguin Modern Classics imprint. Kohli's detailed introductory essay tells us that Kamala Das was born in 1934 into an aristocratic and literary Nair family in the Malabar region of Kerala. She was educated at home and at a European Catholic school in Calcutta, and, at 15, underwent an arranged marriage to an economist and banker working in Bombay, Kalipurayath Madhava Das. Publishing her short stories in 1953, she took the pen-name, Madhavikutty – 'the child-wife of Madhava', to avoid shocking her grandmother with her romantic flights of fancy. It was around this time that she began to write poems in English – the language she chose for all six of her published poetry collections.

Das presents a little self-portrait in another early poem: 'I am Indian, very brown, born in / Malabar, I speak three languages, write in / Two, dream in one.' ('An Introduction'). She goes on to launch her linguistic manifesto, arguing fiercely against the demand that she should write in her Indian mother-tongue: 'Why not let me speak in / Any language I like? The language I speak / Becomes mine, its distortions, its queernesses / All mine, mine alone… It is as human as I am human…' This striking passage is a reminder that Walt Whitman's verse was an important discovery for Kamala Das.

Das's poems often have a forbidden, male muse, but the muse of the American-English language is equally important. It represents her permission to write poetry in free verse, and to write personally, as part of a lived quest to reject subservience and refuse 'to play at pretending games'. The gift for writing unselfconscious autobiography infuses much of her work.

'Someone Else's Song' is not one of her outwardly bold confessional statements: it seems to spring from a mood of uncharacteristic pessimism. The confidence lies, rather, in the understated handling of lyric form. She has found a simple, traditional mould and combines it with a powerful metaphorical language to dramatise women's struggle for autonomy. It's not a typical Das poem, but its existence helps bring her more declarative and formally liberated work into sharper relief.

The incantatory parison of each stanza is introduced by the same assertion, 'I am a million, million'. The sound is both melancholy and lulling, as if the 'million, million', with its childlike shorthand for vast indeterminate quantity, somehow numbed and erased the persona. (The comma suggests that the number has more to do with music than mathematics). To be a million things is overwhelming, and Das is perhaps at her bravest in imagining such a universally multiplied and scattered identity.

The poem's subtler device is a narrative one: the first stanza, essentially, is about voices, the second and third consider death and birth, and the fourth reverses the opening theme, voices, to silences.

It's often in Das's figurative language, rather than in any disruption of syntax, or the rejection of rhyme and metre, where the Indian richness of her English-language writing makes itself felt. Her simile comparing the millions of voices to the noisy chatter of 'maids / At village wells' is bold, simple and effective: suddenly, the millions come alive as individuals. Politically, the plural 'village-wells' is suggestive. This highly literary poet, from a family of poets, must also aspire to 'contain multitudes', like her country and her mentor, and be ready to make things happen in language that's not wholly dependent on educated eloquence. The voices offer possibilities to a writer, but she needs to have control of them and not disappear among them.

The death imagery in the second stanza seems to take the form of pustules which quickly mutate into seed-heads, and, as the image takes hold, become means of an indefinable further life, 'Someday to be shed, to grow for / Someone else, a memory.' In the covert narrative of the poem, death precedes birth, but the trajectory from the vulnerable living voice to its survival through memorial might be a distinctly writerly one. To grow merely for 'someone else', and become a memory, might indicate wasted potential, but it could also imply the glimpse of immortality.

Violent, even shocking images dominate stanza 3. Although the 'births' are 'Flushed with triumphant blood', what is born is a frightening 'Thing' – growing visibly, even as it's being born, its long nails capable of scarring air. This imagery may suggest the goddess Kali. Das, of course, could be imagining these births as metaphors of artistic productions: in that case, how do works of art turn on their creator? Perhaps the answer is that, because they reveal the self, they are susceptible to being used as weapons. Poems may be aggressive political warriors, or simply greedy children, clawing away at their mothers' lives.

Pared-down lines in the final stanza seem to die wistfully on that single word, 'Song'. But perhaps the elegiac shape is another seed that posits a new beginning. The reduction to 'a million, million silences' is complicated, after all, by the transformation of the silences to 'crystal beads'. Although still at the beginning of her career when she wrote this poem, Das already had strong voices in two languages, and knew she could sustain her songs and make them heard. Here she speaks for others as for her more vulnerable self. Their silences, too, are potential points of eloquence. 'Someone Else's Song' is riddled with their questions: the maids at the village-wells are still asking them.

https://www.theguardian.com/books/2015/aug/03/poem-of-the-week-someone-elses-song-by-kamala-das

ZAFFAR KUNIAL

Us

If you ask me, *us* takes in *undulations* –
each wave in the sea, all insides compressed –
as if, from one coast, you could reach out to

the next; and maybe it's a Midlands thing
but when I was young, *us* equally meant *me,*
says the one, 'Oi, you, tell us where yer from';

and the way supporters share the one fate –
I, being one, am *Liverpool* no less –
cresting the Mexican wave of *we* or *us,*

a shore-like state, two places at once, God
knows what's in it; and, at opposite ends
my heart's sunk at separations of *us.*

When it comes to us, colour me unsure.
Something in me, or it, has failed the course.
I'd love to think I could stretch to it – us –

but the waves therein are too wide for words.
I hope you get, here, where I'm coming from.
I hope you're with me on this – between love

and loss – where I'd give myself away, stranded
as if the universe is a matter of one stress.
Us. I hope, from here on, I can say it

and though far-fetched, it won't be too far wrong.

The relaxed vernacular of Kunial's newly published first collection, *Us,* may conceal, on first reading, the highly wrought precision with which his poems search vexations of identity. That theme is explored most plainly in the poem, 'Self-Portrait as Bottom'. Like the title-poem, 'Us', the 'Self-Portrait' references Tony Harrison's forty-year-old sonnet-diptych 'Them and {uz}' (from *The School of Eloquence' and Other Poems,* 1978) in which the sneering literature-teacher tells the working-class Leeds student Harrison, aka T.W, 'You're one of those / Shakespeare gives the comic bits to: prose!'

Kunial's speaker in 'Self-Portrait' refrains from spitting up furious 'glottals': more subtle and contemporary, he dispatches his gobs of spit 'to a lab across the Irish sea' for genetic analysis. The simply complex equation he first announces, '*50% Europe./50% Asia*', demands sub-divisions and further translations, genetic and linguistic, leading to a surprising, tenuous ethnic link between the poet's Kashmir-born father and Midlands-born mother. Themes of disconnection are tacitly present in 'Us'.

'Waves' are a useful metaphor: sea-like waves in the 'undulations' of line 1, develop into the solidarity-asserting action of the 'Mexican wave' in stanza 3. For the football supporter watching a match, such waves emphasise separation, too, 'a shore-like state, two places at once' or a sense of solidarity cut in half: '… and, at opposite ends / my heart's sunk at separations of *us*'. 'Us' means 'me' in many English dialects: Kunial hears it in his native city, Birmingham, in the shout of mixed aggression and curiosity, 'Oi you, tell us where yer from'. In Harrison's 'Them and {uz}', the pronoun symbolises attempts by the ruling 'educated' class to exclude him, but it belongs to the future-poet's own dialect, and he's able to seize the language back ('RIP RP') with a mature, furious confidence not available to Kunial's persona, whose sense of language-rights is less clear-cut. All the same, a quietly intricate assertion of language possession has been set in motion, as modest little phrases like 'the one' and innocent-looking prepositions such as 'from' are slotted quietly into different facets of emphasis.

Difference and familiarity deftly combine in the idiomatic, euphemistic 'colour me unsure'. Now the waves fail to breach distance: the water seems too wide. The speaker hasn't given up, though: repetitions of 'here' demonstrate Kunial's sense of nuance, as if 'here' were no less complicated a verbal sign than 'us' but also as if it could be transformed into identity-grounding solidity. The rough-breathing alliteration of 'hear' and 'hope' gasps uncertainty without checking the smooth rhythmic flow. That image of two shores, two sides, rescues from un-locatable abstraction the territory 'between love and loss'. 'Us' may be the uncertain location of coupledom as well as community, and here, too, the speaker may somehow be undone, given away like a missed goal, 'stranded / as if the universe is a matter of one stress'.

Kunial's puns are never mere play, and here the key word, 'stress', is cleverly chosen. 'Us' as a concept creates stress for those who refuse or are refused belonging. That the single-syllable, two-letter English word could sum up and unite the universe is pressed on the speaker by some further excited vulnerability of doubt and desire ('I hope you're with me on this'). A couple's 'us' seems to extend to the hope, at least, of a broader collective 'us'.

The pronoun has meanwhile shed its italics. Even that typographical shift lends it a more neighbourly look. The resolution gracing this poem turns out to be temporary: the poem immediately following 'Us', a three-part sequence titled 'Ys', painfully searches paths through childhood experiences of disconnection and separation. *Us* provides the collection's title but not Kunial's last word. The irritant which animates his poems, identity, is an interesting compound of connection and disconnection. The two-letter word is less a safely sea-girt island than an undulating, wavily glittering continent. Kunial's 'us' looks outwards, contains multitudes.

https://www.theguardian.com/books/booksblog/2018/jul/02/poem-of-the-week-us-by-zaffar-kunial

ROSS COGAN
Lapstrake

Here you can walk across mudstone and mud
flat, through sedge into a river grown
fat as now, forgetting the tithe of land
taxed from its banks, it ponders borders with
the fierce sea and braids itself to brown
dreadlocks of estuary. Shadowed beneath

an ankle of low cliff is a flat spit
of shale and shingle lent to the windless reach.
Here we can launch. Haul the complaining boat,
breastbone scraping on stone, into the bay;
revive it in water, let its sails catch
the push of air and, filling, pull away.

'Sea kind' the old men call it. With the staves
rolled round their slotted bones then folded in
so side overlies side, they mimic waves'
own lines of rush and fall – at least they do
as well as our loose mapping ever can –
and grip the stream firm as a well-soled shoe

holds snow. The craft that is lapstrake made
turns live to the tiller but still forgives
a clumsy touch. It rests poised as a hand
held palm upwards upon a river's glass
table or treads in diced sea, light as a leaf.
Watch it well. This is the best of us.

‘Lapstrake’ was a word I’d never come across before reading this poem from Ross Cogan’s excellent new collection, *Bragr*. It describes a method of boat building, originating in the Nordic countries, where the edges of the hull-planks, the strakes, overlap each other.

‘Bragr’ is the Old Norse word for ‘poetry’ (the word for ‘poet’, which readers may consider not inappropriate to the species, is *bragi*). Avoiding the pitfall of myth for myth’s sake, Ross Cogan uses Norse characters and fables to drive his major narrative theme, conservation. It was the American biologist, Brian Bowen, who first imagined the connection between the Norse worldview, Orlog, and the three areas most urgently requiring attention if life on earth is to persist, phylogenetics, ecology and evolution.

Observations of human cruelty disturb Cogan’s praise-songs for landscapes, birds and animals (‘Seagulls have fifty-four / different words for anger’ he intriguingly writes elsewhere). The journey is inevitably towards ecological catastrophe, or, in Norse mythic terms, Ragnarök. ‘Lapstrake’, from the book’s first section, ‘The Beginning’, is non-mythological, un-angry, and probably non-hopeful. It describes the harmonious co-operation of man with nature that may only retrospectively represent ‘the best of us’. Although we’re advised to ‘Watch it well’ the lesson may be absorbed too late.

The poem is compelling in the way it mixes the particular and the general. Its first eight lines, for example, are both panoramic and detailed. They picture an estuarial landscape reaching out to and into the sea. The changing negotiations of land and water with one another and the bigger political context evoked in ‘… a river grown / fat as now’ are unfolded in the five and a half lines of the first sentence with little pause for breath. Internal rhymes complicate the flow, like the line-opening full rhymes, ‘flat’ and ‘fat’: there are fainter end-rhymes too (‘grown/brown’, ‘with/beneath’) establishing the stanzaic pattern. The pulse and sound of walking 'across mudstone and mud / flat', the textures of the ground and the river, and the shapes, the 'ankle of low cliff' and the 'flat spit / of shale and shingle' are beautifully synchronised.

So we reach the boat, or the idea of the boat, in the dramatic divisions of the ninth line: 'Here we can launch. Haul the complaining boat, / breastbone scraping on stone, into the bay...' As in the landscape depictions earlier, metaphor tightens the underlying bonds of human bodies and nature. The boat is almost a living creature, and it undergoes transformation. Now we realise it's not a simple rowing-boat but a sailing vessel. Simple, physical diction evokes the thrill of the sails effortlessly filling and the boat, finding its element, slipping out to sea.

The old men's term, 'sea kind', a compound of two plain monosyllables, resembles an Anglo-Saxon kenning. It contains an idea of family kinship with the sea, as well as courtesy towards it – a kind-ness which is returned, since, although lively, 'the craft that is lapstrake made / ... forgives a clumsy touch'.

In the same stanza, the pattern of the staves is seen as wave-like, but, with typical modesty and realism, the narrator acknowledges that 'our loose mapping' allows only a limited imitation of nature. The comparison of the way the staves 'grip the stream' with the way 'a well-soled shoe holds snow' is a great stroke. The use of 'holds' in the sense of 'holds onto' is surprising, and opens up the immediacy of sensation – the wooden staves somehow clinging to the waves, the walker's shoes cutting safely non-slip spaces in heaped snow. The walking image is then taken further, and the craft 'treads in diced sea' although 'light as a leaf'. Throughout the poem, the images and metaphorical associations are close-knit, grounded and appropriate, evoking the ways of a traditional society in an environment it depends on but does not deplete.

It's tempting to see the poem as a work of verbal and rhythmic lapstrake. The six-lined stanzas are never end-stopped, and the rhyming in each stanza, even when full rhyme is used, falls without heavy or strongly schematic insistence. Cogan's emphasis on enjambment suggests the overlap and curvature of lapstrake, and summons the traditions of the poem as craft – craft as in both 'skill' and 'vessel'. It's a distinctly seaworthy piece of work.

https://www.theguardian.com/books/booksblog/2018/aug/06/ poem-of-the-week-lapstrake-by-ross-cogan

VAHNI CAPILDEO

They (may forget (their names (if let out)))

petcitement incitement of a pet to excitement
petcitement incitement into the excitement
of being a pet petcitement incitement to be
a pet a fed pet a fleece pet incitement to be
a floorpet a fleapit a carpet a polkadot
blanket pet blanket pet answer brass doorbell what name
tin waterbowl what name thrilled vomitfall polkadot
padded on patted on turded on welcome mat name
turns to no-one's reminder walks wilder walks further
downriver from calling calling owner predator
who that who tagalong meaner whose canines further
from food fleece floor flea cloth car poll card dot blank bit door
no no owner owns in nomine domini pet
outruns petfetch petcome will wild default reset.

This is a polka-dot pet-blanket of a sonnet, the sonnet as a very gifted, Latin-learned pet might peturb it (sorry). Vahni Capildeo's second collection, *Venus as a Bear*, builds confidently and rangily on an already impressive debut volume, *Measures of Expatriation*. According to the press release for *Venus as a Bear*, Capildeo writes 'on animals, art, language, the sea, thinghood, metaphor, description and dance'. In fact, *all* her poems represent her engagement with language: it's one of the reasons they form such a stimulating reader-space. The idiosyncratic dialect of the current poem is atypical, though.

The poem starts off with a set of variations on the word 'pet' (there are ten 'pets', if you include the word as prefix, in the first six lines), producing a softly crisp percussion of doggy sfx, resembling panting and paw-patter. But 'pet' is a loaded word, and it also asserts the distance of speaker from subject. S/he is only to a degree the pet's ventriloquist. There's a touch of irony, to say the least, in the idea of 'the excitement / of being a pet' and even the repetitive vigour hints at a little human tedium attached to the 'incitement to petcitement'

There's no tedium in the poem itself: it generates constant energy. Canine syntax and rhythm are suggested by the exuberant and pervasive parataxis. The flurry of excitement, the sheer bounce of words on the line and almost off the page, captures at first the essence of affable, tail-wagging pet-dogginess, and, later on, the dog's liberating, unleashed flight from domestic obedience.

The vocal range of the creature is not directly quoted: there are no predictable woofs, yips or growls. Capildeo mixes a Latinate lexicon with words of earthier, more local vintage, words whose root is *citare* (to move) contrasting with the solid 'thinghood' of nouns and compounds like 'floorpet', 'fleapit'. It's enormous fun, especially when the pet answers the door ('What name?') Yes, dogs, like poets, enjoy a bit of naming.

The fun shades off into 'vomitfall' and excrement 'turded on welcome mat' (still fun for the dog, no doubt). Lack of domestic manners has been signalled, and, outdoors, the dog, without resentment, reveals itself as a walker-on-the-wild side. S/he 'walks wilder walks further / downriver from calling calling owner predator'. The syntax deliberately blurs agency, and to paraphrase is to simplify, but among the possible interpretations, the perspective of the pet on its owner is a changed, mistrustful one. The circumscribed domestic-democratic space of 'food fleece floor flea cloth car poll card dot blank bit door' has disappeared like a language learnt but never truly spoken. The inner dog has never been tamed, and now, in an agreeably anthropocentric metaphor, the creature's default is re-set to 'wild'.

So the animal becomes a means of self-interrogation for its owners. What humans have done and still do to the 'animal kingdom' is a history we insufficiently acknowledge. Even the poem's title recognises this: the virtues of obedience are interrogated in the Olson-like parentheses, in which terms of imprisonment are almost visually captured. The pets' names are not really theirs, the domesticity is enforced. (if let out))) implies they only *might* be let out: they might be chained. The dog that finds its own open field, and 'outruns petfetch petcome', has sniffed enslavement; by reverting 'to nature' it becomes politically exemplary.

In the tumbling quadruped-biped dance of Capildeo's sonnet, in the swirl of multiple meanings and moods, the ambivalence and falseness of animal/human relations are undoubtedly registered. There is no right of pet-ownership, no God-given authority, even if the power is scaffolded by Latin formulae like 'in nomine domini' (in the name of the lord). When the dog gets wind of its own feral nature, and turns with the sonnet's major 'turn' into a free being, there's a sense that an injustice has been put right. Is there also a lingering question as to whether the simple reversal of power can deliver justice?

https://www.theguardian.com/books/booksblog/2018/may/21/poem-of-the-week-they-may-forget-their-names-if-let-out-by-vahni-capildeo

SYL CHENEY-COKER

The Colour of Stones

I

When you arrive in this misnamed country,
come to the crooked hills; the fierce, verdant eyes
of Sierra Leone, mythic songs, its crazy history!
Named in limestone – Wilberforce, Regent,
Leicester, Gloucester and Charlotte – the old,
smoky villages of deft colonials and benefactors
are dying. Quarried with ruin now, they were once
the crown jewels of English Christian love.

II

Under the tamarind, the gowned-women in kabaslot[1]
are shy, but still invite young men to their modest homes.
They dim the paraffin lamps, offer sweet fibers of ginger,
the sorrel fragrance of golden days, and move their lips,
as though under the magic of the Gambian herb, with which
the Aku women[2] once tempted the mouths of Christian lovers.

III

The secrets of golden age, entombed in the old grannies'
bones, have turned gray; but they shimmer and refuse
the eternal death stamp. Fiery lianas, they twine round
the bodies of the young, philistine ploughmen, who are
reckless with adzes. Ah, those beloved grannies, eternal
and watching, as new arrogance drapes their smoking hills,
which will never die – always alive – this mountain country!

---

1 *Kabaslot* – gown worn by Sierra Leonean women

2 *Aku women* – Moslem women

Syl Cheney-Coker was born in the Sierra Leonean capital, Freetown, in 1945. He completed his education in the USA, and, after further travels, went on to be a Visiting Writer at the International Writing Programme of the University of Iowa. He returned to Sierra Leone, but was later among the writers forced into exile for criticising the one-party government. These days, he spends time in both countries, the USA and Sierra Leone. 'I believe my poems have always been linked by three common themes', he writes: 'the awakening of my identity; the pain of exile, and a basic concern for those whose humanity is sometimes threatened by others'.

The Author's Note in his latest collection recounts the following story. A small publisher in the US many years ago had been interested in bringing out the volume, but the young writer hesitated. 'Deeply aware of my dual identity, I felt the poems, as a whole, were immature, too Senghorian; but without his splendid beauty. Two of the poems were absorbed into *Concerto for an Exile*, after which I tore up the rest of the volume.'

Thirty-seven years later, an ex-girlfriend from college sent Cheney-Coker a packet: inside it, the copy of the collection, intact. It was a gift he'd forgotten all about. She wrote, 'I think you might enjoy reading these poems after all these years.' Pleased, but still cautious, he put the poems away for another four years. Finally, eight of the twenty poems, much revised, became the first part of the 2015 edition of *The Road to Jamaica*. Part Two contains his more recent work, under the title *Elegy for the Afro-Saxon*. 'The Colour of Stones' is one of these poems.

The term 'Afro-Saxon' denotes a person of African descent with English or Anglo-American affiliations. Perhaps Sierra Leonean culture is particularly diverse and open to such complexity? Among the many ethnic groups, the Krio are the descendants of the freed slaves, after whom Freetown was named, and they continue to reflect Western cultural influences. There are references to Muslims and Christians in the poem, to 'colonials and benefactors', to the indigenous 'beloved old grannies' and the 'young, philistine ploughmen who are / reckless with adzes'. The mountainous country seems to have come through its 'crazy history' to an accommodation with different people, different times.

An easy, colloquial style combines with mellow timbres. The adjective 'verdant' in line 2 implies more than the colour green; it encompasses rainy lushness and ripeness, a quality audible in the rich descriptive textures of the second stanza, in particular: 'tamarind', 'paraffin lamps', 'sweet fibers of ginger', 'sorrel fragrance'. Gold, the predominant colour, suggests colonial plunder and 'misnaming' but, also, the mythical Golden Age, the 'golden days' of lovers, and the 'secrets' of the indomitable grannies' 'golden age'. These secrets are preserved in the bones of the old women and 'shimmer and refuse the eternal death stamp'. The spondee 'death stamp' with its hard flat sounds suddenly recalls the bureaucratic processes of oppression, when imprisonment, death-sentence or asylum-refusal are inked indelibly on the official piece of paper. But it's a passing memory.

'The Colour of Stones' evokes a rainbow coalition. The tone is warm, seemingly amused by divergence and transgression. In the second stanza, the Aku women have 'tempted the mouths of Christian lovers' with a special herb: perhaps the aphrodisiac Kola Nut? All the humans beings in the poem seem at ease with themselves and each other, and 'the other'. There is no elevation of a single ethnicity, but there is deeply loving patriotism – or should that be 'matriatism'?

'{T}this misnamed country' is thought, probably incorrectly, to have been given its name by the Portuguese explorer, Pedro de Sintra. 'Sierra Leone' derives from 'Serra Lyoa' (lioness mountains). Was it so-called because of the shape of the hills?

'Serra' means 'a series of mountains or saw-like ridge'. The name might allude to the lioness's opened mouth and bared teeth.

Gently, Cheney-Coker takes back his homeland, initially re-shaping the hills, very simply, as 'crooked'. As he descends among 'the old / smoky villages' he uncovers only ruins, and those absurd, out-of-place, yet almost naturalised English place-names, denoting, once, 'the crown jewels of English Christian love'. From there on, fertility, warmth and feminine energy flow through the poem's conduits, and the poet claims his soul-landscape with a cry of triumph. These 'smoking hills' may now be threatened by deforestation, mining or other industries, but, in his loving imagination, they are indestructible: 'always alive – this mountain country!'

https://www.theguardian.com/books/booksblog/2019/feb/11/poem-of-the-week-the-colour-of-stones-by-syl-cheney-coker

ROBERT SHEPPARD

Prison Camp Violin, Riga

A brittle fiddle someone
Turns this on a lathe

Of the spheres where
Replica becomes the real

Thing thin
Birch treated knocked up

Catches an unhuman
Voice in its hollow

Thumbs moulded to pegs
Skewered into splitting holes

Tune the stolen wires a
Mollusc curled at neck's end

Fingernails
Pluck the kinked tune free

Out of itself a
Collapsed bridge

Sabotaged by
Time mittens

Grapple
The soup-bone bow-grip

Horse hair human
Hair taut straight like a well

Brushed bride’s
Bends the tamed twig

Tucked under your chin the violin
Splinters against your jaw

As you draw the grinty
Voice out from the mechanics

Of survival: extinct
Livonian love song.

‘Prison Camp Violin, Riga’ (from *History or Sleep: Selected Poems* by Robert Sheppard) appears online in the group of ‘Three Riga Poems’ headed ‘Metzendorff House, Riga’, where it’s sub-grouped as the first poem of a ‘Riga Duet’ (the second being ‘Mute Piano’).

The poem is always peopled, and the violin is always vocal. It doesn’t start only with the object itself, the ‘brittle fiddle’, but its manufacture by an unidentified ‘someone’. The ‘lathe // Of the spheres where / Replica becomes the real // Thing’ gives breathing space to the enormity of hope in such a context and the vastness beyond the prison camp boundaries: ‘spheres’ can’t but suggest ‘the music of the spheres’. In contrast, the fiddle’s ‘thin / Birch treated knocked up’ is frail, cheap and false, like prison-life, which is only available as a ‘replica’ of living. The use of ‘unhuman’ to describe the ‘voice’ makes clear the distinction between the violin voice, a painful, ghostly wonder, and the inhuman voices surrounding it. Being 'caught', the voice could, equally, be that of the violinist. This presence, now stringing and tuning the instrument, is evoked in the brutal, torture-evoking physicality of 'Thumbs moulded to pegs / Skewered into splitting holes'. Always in process, the violin is an object being shaped, played and controlled, as is the prison or concentration-camp inmate. At the same time, there are moments when it's held descriptively still, as in the metaphor of 'a / Mollusc curled at neck's end'. Even then, we might think of the playing hand as well as the wooden scroll.

Now 'Fingernails / Pluck the kinked tune free…', but the bridge, both violin-part and metaphorical bridge, and also, perhaps, 'the kinked tune' itself, has been 'Sabotaged by / Time mittens'. Those muffling 'm' sounds silence the pizzicato. The pause is only temporary: these same mittens, resurgent, manage to 'Grapple / The soup-bone bow-grip'.

To make a violin and its bow, once living organisms have to become, or yield, commodities. A seeming glimpse elegant and glossy bourgeois ceremonies ('Horse hair human / Hair taut straight like a well / Brushed bride's') contrasts with the 'soup-bone bow-grip' and 'tamed twig' which constitute the bare, elemental shapes of terminal deprivation. 'Human hair' is a phrase which can't possibly escape contamination in such a context, and isn't meant to.

'Prison Camp Violin', Riga evolves into a tribute to the unknown player. The concluding three couplets talk to him or her, imagined, in a gentle, familiar way, to still lodge the fiddle under the chin. The solo continues: notice all those short 'i' sounds, emphasising once more the brittleness and thinness of the 'knocked up' object and the dereliction from which the melody gains temporary reprieve. Sent back to stanza 3 for another view of the poem's beginnings, I remembered the 'street' meaning of 'knocked up' (made pregnant). 'Grinty' may be another slang term: the Urban Dictionary offers a range of definitions of 'grint', among them, abusive shorthand for immigrant. As an adjective qualifying the 'voice', 'grinty' is onomatopoeic, and has the strained, edgy, tinny sound of a tune drawn 'out from the mechanics // Of survival'. This voice in the final couplet shocks us freshly, unexpectedly summoning further dereliction, the extinguished language and nation of Livonia.

In 'the new sentence' as defined by Ron Silliman, the prose paragraph organises its sentences into 'a unit of quantity, not logic or argument'. In Prison Camp Violin, Riga, it's the clauses of the single poem-long sentence which work this way, continually making new paths across the boundaries which grammar, line and stanza are prone to enforce. Interpretations are only passing connections in a shape-shifting syntactical flux, where noun quickly changes into adjective, object into subject. Sustaining and controlling the multiplication of possible meanings, Sheppard connects lyric into narrative, blends units of time and space. Sonic effects give the poem the violin's own voice, its timbre and its music. The text itself, although in motion, holds its shape.

https://www.theguardian.com/books/booksblog/2018/jul/23/poem-of-the-week-prison-camp-violin-riga-by-robert-sheppard

MALIKA BOOKER

Sin Visits Me

They say a dead woman can't run from her coffin.
How moonshine can orchestrate nuff wild thoughts!
It's an hour past midnight and the road outside is quiet;
my thoughts are a twisting screwdriver; licks
of a dozen switches scorch my skin. Pomegranate flowers
line the road, each spread out from the other,
and their crumpled petals are the shocking red of death.
I am in the centre of this wreath. You chew chillies raw,
laugh, and spit the seeds, then tell me of the joys
of sitting on a big stone under Concord waterfall,
watching near-naked boys leap off the moss-green cliffs above.
Your voice is smooth liquor. Your whirring hands speak
another language. I hold a white china cup in my hand;
funny how the cracks don't seem to show.
You in your saucy lace that binds your body like mace
covers nutmeg seeds; I am shocked by your vulgarity.
I tell you, crapaud don't have no right in salt water.
You tell me you have a right to be everywhere.

The 'wild thoughts' relished in 'Sin Visits Me' mix place, memory, erotic dream and ghost-story. Malika Booker, 'raised in London soil and Guyana sun', chooses a Grenada setting here, as for many of the poems in her first collection *Pepper Seed*. The book contains a number of poignant elegies, but 'Sin Visits Me' refuses the conventional sadness and consolation of the genre: it faces death with a bold and even joyous insouciance.

Under the admitted influence of 'moonshine' – which could be moonlight or alcohol or both – the speaker conjures the dead woman, the poem's addressee, up and out of her coffin, acknowledging that she might be fantasising ('nuff wild thoughts') but willing to suspend disbelief. The death may have been a violent one, and the mourner's initial grief is intense, as references to thoughts resembling 'a twisting screwdriver' and skin scorched by 'licks / of a dozen switches' suggest. The pomegranate flowers are menacing, too; encroaching, somehow, despite the 'crumpled petals' and forming a linked chain, they're 'the shocking red of death', and the speaker positions herself 'in the centre of this wreath'. But from the point at which the dead woman is encountered, the exchange becomes lively and intimate. The speaker switches to the vocative. The ghost laughs and begins by describing her un-ghostly relish for watching the 'near-naked boys' leaping into the waterfall.

She's a woman identified with sexuality, and therefore 'sin'. She may be demonic. Her 'whirring hands' and even the 'saucy lace' she wears could suggest the scaly, winged body of some beautiful non-human creature, a kind of Lamia. Caribbean folklore has its own sexy, beautiful, female demon, La Diablesse.

Both the whirring hands and the cracked china cup are images which recall Auden's ballad, 'As I Walked Out one Evening'. There, the clocks begin to 'whirr and chime', and 'the crack in the teacup opens / A lane to the land of the dead'.

Auden's protagonist is threatened by the passage of time and his unfulfilled sexual needs. If Booker is borrowing those images it's to challenge their implicit boundaries. The cracks in the cup are invisible because there is no need for lanes opening into the land of the dead: it's where the poem is set.

At no time does the dead woman pose a threat to the speaker. Her voice is 'smooth liquor'. She's at ease with herself, a role model of sturdy independence and sensuality, steeped in the red of pomegranate flowers, blood, and sex, as she chews raw chilli peppers and spits the seeds. Taste will again be evoked, with an internal rhyme to press the simile home, in that jokily admiring observation: 'You in your saucy lace that binds your body like mace / covers nutmeg seeds.' The presence of spices and seeds suggests celebratory meals, love-feasts. The woman may be the peppery 'seed' of Malika Booker's inspiration.

The poem's speaker is a lively character, too. She answers back, she teases the ghost. Caesuras give bounce to her speech. There's amusement in her manner. When she says she's shocked by the woman's vulgarity, the irony is obvious: not only is she not shocked, she's charmed.

Patois is sparingly used, appearing only in the second and penultimate lines. Initially, it suggests the speaker's self-mockery: finally, it adds zest to a brilliant bit of dialogue between her and La Diablesse: 'I tell you, crapaud don't have no right in salt water. / You tell me you have a right to be everywhere.'

I thought the 'crapaud' line might be based on an actual proverb. A list of Trinidad 'sayings' yielded 'Crapaud smoke your pipe' and 'Cockroach have no right to fowl party' – both evoking occasions of non-human insolence. Toads are associated with magic and transformation, but, as a derogatory term for Frenchman, 'crapaud' is also a reminder of a stage in a much contested island's colonisation. And it cues the dead woman into a strong retort.

The 'right to be everywhere' might have asserted the ubiquity of death, but it seems instead to be a joyous expression of a free spirit. The ghost needed death to find liberation, perhaps, but the speaker realises that she can seize it here. The poem is that act of seizing life.

https://www.theguardian.com/books/booksblog/2017/may/15/poem-of-the-week-sin-visits-me-by-malika-booker

IAN GREGSON

Squawks and Speech

Only the parrot observes
his body beside the futon where he tumbled.
Hello, she calls, and again *Hello* -
a voice on a cut-off phone -
and *Come Back Peter*,

calls as though to the voices
and music from downstairs of the lonely TV,
or blackbird near the window where words
extend themselves through the wire
under its solo.

She perches on the spread map
on the table, squawks, and waddles into the sea
off Anglesey, her *Come Back Peter*
as though she's searching for where
he might be really.

Her hunger surprises her,
the cold withering of habitat that started
when Peter changed from upright to flat -
a tree in the rainforest
that echoes briefly,

thunders across silent miles
then joins the endless cycle of decay and growth.
But Peter stays the same, as rush hours
pass him by both ways, and buses
circle around him.

Most days the door's beak opens
and emits, not cries, but letters and newspapers
that sprawl in heaps like speech that tumbles
from a mouth onto the ground
unheard and lies there -

echolalia from outside
repeating his name as though trying to recall
Peter, who he is, and how he fits
into the network of roads -
he's a missing piece,

lost in a room like a mind
with a memory that over and over returns,
a phrase that recurs and calls his name
in a tone that's not his own -
a stuck interior

where the clock is sweeping through
a single season though pollen now is mingling
with the dust on its face, and sunlight
edges across Peter's brow.
The year is tilting

and Peter's eyes are open
so the cat returning squints and mews at his lit
irises, while, buffeting the casement,
gusts cry their one syllable
of a cross baby.

'Squawks and Speech' is a vivid and disconcerting narrative from Ian Gregson's 2008 collection, *How We Met*. It appears in the first of three sections, entitled 'Sideways at the War'. As the neighbouring poems attest, 'war' is defined in the widest metaphorical sense of social fracture and fragmentation. War includes the city's chaos, the loss of human connection and the dislocated individual consciousness.

The protagonist, Peter, seems to have died suddenly at home. We're told few details about him, but enough to piece together a basic outline. We know he's affluent and sophisticated enough to own a futon and an exotic bird. The map left open on the table suggests he might have been anticipating a journey. When the poem begins, he has already been dead, or possibly comatose, for some time, and as it continues, the extent of his isolation becomes clear. The only witness, apart from the narrator, is Peter's parrot.

The syllabic structure of the stanzas (7,12,9,7,5) conveys a narrative movement of fits and starts and circles – an endless, unresolvable movement which is also that of the bird. Absence of communication is ironised by the fact that the bird can speak, i.e. she has picked up a small, human vocabulary, which she uses as though to communicate with other voices (sounds from a downstairs TV, the blackbird outside on the telegraph wire) and to call her owner (*Come Back Peter)*. The mimicked words mean nothing to the bird, or rather, their human meaning is lost in a repertoire of nuanced squawks. Her '*Come Back Peter*' may be copied from the children's game, or perhaps picked up from someone who was once intimate with Peter: it hints at lively interactions long since abandoned. The 'spread map', showing the island of Anglesey, sharpens the pathos of Peter's immobility and the bird's busy helplessness. In a moment of painful comedy, in which communication systems overlap incomprehensibly, she perches on the map, 'squawks and waddles into the sea'.

The parrot's perspective is laced into the narrative from stanza 4. Without human language, she still knows hunger and anguish – 'the cold withering of habitat'. She perceives that the man has 'changed from upright to flat' and that 'the door's beak opens' to issue newspapers and letters. The parrot reads Peter's human world in *parrot.* While her alienation from her natural habitat is evoked, the poem finds an unexpected similarity between her situation and that of Peter. His corpse, which resembles, for the parrot, a fallen tree, is also outside 'the endless cycle of decay and growth'.

The perspective seems to shift slightly but mysteriously in stanza 8. The room itself, caging voices and words which never find response or meaning, is compared to a mind, which might almost be Peter's mind, as if he were trying to put himself back together. Again, the stasis of the 'stuck interior' and repetitive echo contrasts with a widening arc of movement. From the earlier flow of city traffic to the seasonal change and 'tilting' in the penultimate stanza, wave-like motion surrounds the islanded man (whose name, of course, derives from 'rock'.) A cat, which comes and goes on its own inscrutable business, is the last uncomprehending witness, disturbed by the glare of Peter's eyes, but no more able to find a language of communication than the weather – those 'gusts' at the end of the poem which deceptively 'cry their one syllable / of a cross baby'.

'Squawks and Speech' seems at times surreal in its speedy juxtapositions. Its images are so organised that external things, like the buses and roads, seem part of the interior setting. As the key simile, 'a room like a mind', suggests, the narrative is not only concerned with fractured external connections but those inherent to perception. How do we complete the jigsaw of self-knowledge when there are so many dead echoes, so many voices which name us without knowing who we are? The image of Peter's eyes, wide open and lit from without, brings a frisson of the uncanny to a poem that has never settled comfortably for a single tone, but has succeeded in juggling pathos and comedy, lyricism and narrative, in its constantly broken and remade syllabic web.

https://www.theguardian.com/books/2014/jul/21/ squawks-and-speech-ian-gregson-poem-of-the-week

SIOBHAN CAMPBELL

Origin of the Mimeo

What do guns when they are not in use?
In the dead of night they double and divide,
naming new owners, finding a new ruse.

Carry a gun on stage, it must be fired.
Deterrent only lasts until undone.
Better they are counted out of mind.

List the ways to frame a decommission,
a car-park graveyard covered with cement.
Which stay on stasis is sufficient?

Marking each as *put beyond use.*
Keeping their provenance as you would art.
Rocking the replicas back to their false start.
It's got to be efficient.

A suggestive metaphor from thermal imaging technology provides the title of Siobhán Campbell's new collection, *Heat Signature,* and sustains its resonance in 'Origin of the Mimeo'.

The invention of the mimeograph, an early copying machine, dates back to the nineteenth century. It was supplanted by the photocopier some time ago. But the reader doesn't need to remember the mimeograph to get the reference, since imitation (as in mime) is spelled out in the word itself, and emphasised in its cohabitation with 'original'. The double summoning of the past, including the recent past, is surely apt.

Campbell's larger focus is the contemporary 'matter of Ireland'. Unusually, there's little sense of a north-south border, or at least one that can't be freely trampled. The Dublin-born Campbell seems comfortable with the uncomfortable, a native not of the south or north but of the problematic, including the Peace Process and its vicissitudes. This poem challenges assumptions about the value of de-commissioning. Replication undermines the pledge to put a weapon 'beyond use' (line 10 quotes the formula) and mocks the burial: the dead weapon in its 'carpark graveyard' proliferates. These guns are not only undead: they 'double and divide'.

Terseness predominates in Campbell's syntax as the phrasing of the opening questions signals: not 'What do guns do when they're not in use' but 'What do guns when they're not in use'. This archaic, possibly Hiberno-English idiom emphasises the guns' sparky animation. The weapon has a sinister life of its own, and can find its own combatants and reasons for use. The rhyming of 'use' and ruse' is eloquent.

The second stanza introduces Chekhov's famous dictum, 'One must never place a loaded rifle on the stage if it isn't going to go off. It's wrong to make promises you don't mean to keep', and broadens the poem's frame of reference. Campbell herself, in her creative-critical thesis *From There to Here: Writing out of a time of violence,* reads 'Origin of the Mimeo' as a poem about poetry. Chekhov's rule highlights the contract of author and auditor, and could apply to any significant object, and to other literary genres than drama. The rule might be extended to embarrass the concept of the weapon as a deterrent – if it exists, it will be used. But Campbell is interested in the question at the level of this specific poem: having introduced the gun 'onto the stage of the poem', is she obliged to fire it?

Campbell's lines are mostly in trochaic pentameter; they are orderly, never leisurely. Her single sentence, single line statements are perhaps meant to be verbal gunshots. Or perhaps it's the curtailed last line which fires the gun.

In stanza 2 the moral clincher of the third line plays on the verb in apposition, 'counted out' and its transformation into 'counted out of mind'. Previously, the italics of *deterrent* remind us of a word claiming too much for itself.

In the third stanza the idea of the list is raised and mocked by the image of 'a carpark graveyard covered with cement'. There are too many ways to 'frame a decommission', beginning with the interpretation of 'frame', no doubt. The phrase has an odd echo of Elizabeth Barratt Browning counting the ways of love, possibly hinting at Campbell's resistance to lyric sentimentality.

Lyrical grace may be suspect, the terza rima casually plaited, but there's an energy in the language, buried metaphors, gleams of word-play that are more than mere lace ('stay on stasis', 'rocking the replicas back to their false start'). The latter is particularly interesting. Campbell points out the Yeats connection with 'rocking' in her thesis: presumably it's primarily 'The Second Coming' which is invoked.

Only the decommissioning of the mind will put the gun beyond use. Meanwhile, the very word 'gun' is potent, a disturbing image in three coiled letters. Perhaps the poem itself is mimetic, a small, loaded object with underground connections, its own forms of subterfuge and escape.

The thought is often complex. To keep a gun's provenance 'as you would art' suggests the placing of high value on the original. This may of course be an allusion to historical responsibility. In 'rocking the replicas back to their false start' it's the term 'false start' which suggests the possibility of beginning afresh.

The throw-away last line can be read in several ways. It looks back at the earlier lines of the quatrain, that powerful triad of gerunds which answered the command to 'list the ways to frame a decommission': 'Marking each as *put beyond use.* / Keeping their provenance as you would art. / Rocking the replicas back to their false start.') And, grammatically, the pronoun 'it's' refers to the 'stay on stasis'. There's a complicating idiomatic twist in the line. 'It's got to be efficient' can mean 'it's sure to be efficient' or 'it will need to be efficient'. Then there's the (attractive) potential for irony: 'none of this is at all efficient'. The poem is too finely balanced to decommission either optimism or pessimism.

https://www.theguardian.com/books/booksblog/2017/sep/18/ poem-of-the-week-origin-of-the-mimeo-by-siobhan-campbell

MIMI KHALVATI

Everywhere you see her…

Everywhere you see her, who could have been
  Monet's woman with a parasol
who's no woman at all but an excuse for wind –
  passage of light-and-shade we know
wind by – just as his pond was no pond
  but a globe at his feet turning to show
how the liquid, dry, go topsy-turvy, how far
  sky goes down in water. Like iris, agapanthus
waterplants from margins where, tethered
  by their cloudy roots, clouds grow underwater
and lily-floes, like landing craft, hover
  waiting for departure, she comes at a slant
to crosswinds, currents, against shoals of sunlight
  set adrift, loans you her reflection.
I saw her the other day I don't know where
  at a tangent to some evening, to a sadness
she never shares. She wavers, like recognition.
  Something of yours goes through her, something
of hers escapes. To hillbrows, meadows
  where green jumps into her skirt, hatbrim shadows
blind her. To coast, wind at her heels, on diagonals
  as the minute hand on the hour, the hour
on the wheel of sunshades. Everywhere you see her.
  On beaches, bramble paths, terraces of Edwardian
hotels. In antique shops, running her thumb along
  napworn velvet. A nail buffer. An owl brooch
with two black eyes of onyx. Eyes she fingers.
  But usually on a slope. Coming your way.

This week's poem is by Mimi Khalvati, one of my favourite contemporary poets and also the subject of a 'special request' from one of our recent 'Poem of the Week' posters, Poulter. I've made my choice from Khalvati's 1997 collection, *Entries on Light*, a book-length sequence of poems, all untitled, all subtly linked. They are both mystical and down-to-earth, innovative and approachable, precise in visual detail but roomy in vision. However well you may know the work, there is always something fresh to discover there. If you're new to it, this poem ('Everywhere you see her…') will, I hope, be a good starting point.

The word 'Entries' suggests a diary, and, though meticulously crafted, the poems reflect the variations of a typical English calendar, quick-firing through light, shade and the whole chromatic scale between. Someone has pointed out a resemblance to Constable's paintings; up to a point, that's true, provided we remember that Constable was not simply a narrator, and his light was more than physical light. Khalvati's poems are only passingly descriptions or records. In showing us 'what the light was like' they show us how it felt, what memories were roused, how it read emotionally and intellectually. As well as water and sky, rooms and hillsides, we see how light plays on the 'inward eye' – the poet's imagination.

Although Khalvati's work is steeped in English tradition (Herbert and Wordsworth are presences here), the shaping of the sequence signals her deep connection with Persian poetry. Edwin Morgan, who wrote his own, marvellous 'take' on Middle Eastern poetry in *The New Divan* (1977), described the open structure, and the sensation of exploring it: 'In Arabic or Persian poetry they're rather fond of the idea that a "divan" as they call it, a collection of poems, is something you enter; you move around, you can cast your eye here and there, you look, you pick, you perhaps retrace your steps.' (*Nothing Not*

Giving Messages). There are myriad 'entries' into, and passages through, Khalvati's sequence.

The poem I've chosen is a mysterious, impressionistic portrait, related to Monet's windswept figure of the 'Woman with a Parasol'. It's not 'about' the Monet paintings, but the allusion helps us visualise the strange, dissolving quality of the poem's central image. 'Everywhere you see her' could signal a love-poem, obsessed by a particular woman. Equally, it could be about 'Everywoman'. Her identity is unstable, because the weather of the receptive imagination constantly re-shapes it. Monet himself painted two women with parasols – his wife and, later, his step-daughter. Khalvati's figure, like Monet's, seems at first to be composed of sky and wind. She's also kin to the rippling water-plants of the lily-pond, and to water itself: like a bird, she coasts 'on diagonals'. (I read 'coast' as a verb as well as a noun). She might have slipped out of an Irish Aisling poem. Although hardly an emblem of nationhood, she seems, like the 'sky-woman' of the genre, a muse-figure. Perhaps she is poetry. Perhaps she is the light in human form.

The fluidity of her identity at the beginning suggests a parallel with the dawning of a poem. As her outline becomes clearer, and analogies accumulate, it's like seeing a poem take shape. 'Something of yours goes through her, something / of hers escapes.' This is a wonderfully suggestive picture of the creative transaction, and maybe of perception in general. But the woman is soon to be grounded: her insistent hat-brim and her dallying among antiques lend her a worldly air, a place in society and time.

The poem 's syntax changes to accompany the theme's development. Sinuous long sentences, with carefully timed line-breaks adding their own punctuation (Khalvati sometimes uses the line-ending as the grammatical equivalent of the comma) give way to brisker units, not always complete sentences. Towards the end of the poem, a movement of stops and starts produces the sense of hunting, dodging, hide-and-seek. Is the speaker the hunter, or the hunted?

Another Celtic hint recalls the Mabinogion, and the tale in which Blodeuwedd, a bride conjured by wizardry from the flowers of the oak, the broom and the meadow-sweet, is punished for marital treachery by demotion to an owl. The owl in this poem is only a brooch, but it has a piercing presence. The black eyes the woman 'fingers' are senseless and lightless, hinting at the inhumanity of the greedily absorbent, unreflective surfaces of art.

Finally, the woman is freed from the claustrophobic Old Curiosity Shop where the poet has mischievously deposited her, and set again on the timeless hillside that is her element. But the idea that she is 'on a slope' and 'coming your way' continues to mingle notions of the predatory and playful. Her arrival in the flesh could mean anything from an epiphany to a catastrophe – possibly both. If she's inspiration, then she is the poet's most difficult of guests, as well as most welcome.

https://www.theguardian.com/books/booksblog/2011/jun/27/ poem-of-the-week

NAOMI FOYLE

Your Summer Arm

Was it an odd sort of cricket
climbing my oak dresser? No –
an emerald shield bug, you said,
watching as I tried to slide

a piece of A4 paper
beneath its crooked legs.
When a foot caught, and tore,
I thought we both might cry.

*

Where is grass to comfort that green?
Those sweet, young shoots
I slipped from their sheaths
and chewed with wobbly teeth?

Now, as we curl into bed,
outside in the whistling damp
the husk I dismembered today
begins to decay in the leaves.

*

This whirring of thoughts,
rustle of pages,
mean nothing to you
anymore.

Your breathing is so quiet
I'd hardly know you were there
if it wasn't for the glowing limb
buried in my hair.

How do the approaches of men and women to writing contemporary love-poetry differ? Is the representation of double-sided couple instead of lone lyricist-and-distant-muse a particularly female preoccupation?

From *The Night Pavilion*, a lively first collection by Naomi Foyle, 'Your Summer Arm' comes from the third, title section of the book. It concludes a series of poems influenced by Emily Dickinson's hymn-like forms, creating, in the writer's words, 'incantations or "failed" hymns' that seek 'to re-forge the connection between sexuality and the sacred'. It traces a further duality, the likeminded-ness of the lovers, and the differences. There is no quarrel between them but the speaker's interior world creates a disturbing room-within-a-room.

The room is identified early on as the speaker's ('my oak dresser'). At first, the couple have a conversation about the species of the invading insect: it brings them together, even though the one addressed corrects the other's questioning proposition: 'Was it an odd sort of cricket?' Trying to 'rescue' the emerald shield-bug on a sheet of A4 paper, the speaker damages its delicate foot. Both the humans are upset ('I thought we both might cry') but it's the speaker whose memory remains haunted by the dismemberment, and who, in the poem's second section imagines the unidentified husk – that of the beetle, but perhaps a premonition of disappointment in the relationship in the relationship.

The two characters neatly complement each other: one's uncertainty is the other's capability. The addressee knows the insect's name, but can't help practically. The speaker, for all her finesse, fatally damages the insect. These tiny events gain powerful significance in such a context. The lovers remain tentative and seem themselves at risk. They tread very carefully and find points of cohesion along the way, near-resolutions echoed in the far-apart para-rhymes linking the last lines of each pair of quatrains.

It will be obvious by now that the natural world that frames the lovers in this poem is not the conventional one. The insect that is out of place on the oak dresser is also quite a 'foreign body' in poetry. It makes an effective symbol for poetry itself (fine structures and surprising movements), and connects us to the processes of thinking and writing, with the sheet of A4 on which it's captured and, audibly, the 'whirring of thoughts' and 'rustle of pages'.

The poem both takes things apart and looks for salves and solutions. It becomes a love-poem the moment we learn that the couple, whatever they may not share, share the emotion over the hurt bug. But the speaker's pained rhetorical question, 'Where is grass to comfort that green?' is privately uttered and the childhood memory of vulnerable milk-teeth and sweet-tasting grass is another question rather than an answer. Fragmentation occurs not only in the narrative: it's present in the title itself (not arms, but 'arm', singular) and the three-part structure, which conveys visual and rhythmic segmentation.

Finally, the lovers' separateness is reconciled. The visually arresting image of a lover's 'glowing limb' covered by the other's hair announces that the pair are united in a relaxed, sleepy warmth, both sexual and companionable. So one-ness is almost attained – but not quite. 'Limb' and 'hair' have utterly different functions and textures, almost as different as those of the oak dresser and the fragile, crooked-legged insect. The arm itself is a vulnerable limb, and reminds us of the unlucky shield bug, its body now buried in leaves. And only one of the couple is peacefully asleep. The other is awake, and observing – eternally vigilant, as the writer has to be, looking in, looking out, trying to name the world and make sense without loss of mystery.

Foyle succeeds in her ambition to combine sacred and sexual. We know that the lovers' paradise is now flawed by death, but the greenness and glow of summer and life continue: the lover, breathing almost silently, is only asleep, and the presence of the glowing 'summer arm' is what remains in the speaker's consciousness, and ours, at the end of the poem. A gentle rhyme, 'there' and 'hair' underlines the physical harmony of the lovers in their sleeping/waking embrace.

https://www.theguardian.com/books/booksblog/2008/nov/24/poem-week-summer-arm-foyle

W.S. GRAHAM

How Are the Children Robin

for Robin Skelton

It does not matter how are you how are
The children flying leaving home so early?
The song is lost asleep, the blackthorn breaks
Into its white flourish. The poet walks
At all odd times hoping the road is empty.
I mean me walking hoping the road is empty.

Not that I would ever expect to see
Them over the brow of the hill coming
In scarlet anoraks to meet their Dad.
A left, a right, my mad feet trudge the road
Between the busy times. It raineth now
Across the hedges and beneath the bough.

It does not matter let that be a lesson
To cross the fields. Keep off the roads. The Black
Wood of Madron with its roof of rooks
Is lost asleep flying into the dusk.
When shall we see the children older returning
Into the treetops? And what are they bringing?

'Something to do with the generation gap, in a kind of way', W.S. Graham once mused, after reading 'How Are the Children Robin' to an audience. That recording is online, and it's essential listening if you don't yet have the unique Graham sound in your head. The hard-edged enunciation, as if each word were being printed, letterpress-style, onto silence, and the pauses between word and word and line and line which make that silence audible, are integral to the poem's meanings. Graham's rhotic accent informs the entire song of it, while adding special intensity to such lines as 'The Black / Wood of Madron with its roof of rooks'. The modesty, pride and humour of Graham's asides are delightful extras.

Graham was born in 1918 in Greenock on the Firth of Clyde and began his working life as a structural engineer, before moving south and settling ultimately in the Cornish village Madron, named in this poem and many others. There he enjoyed friendship and creative exchange with a number of the St Ives painters. He died in January 1986.

Graham famously began writing under the influence of Dylan Thomas. Most critics take the view that he found his own pitch and style only after distancing his work from 'the Welsh wizard'. However, Thomas's influence was digested rather than discarded, nourishing the treatment of language as promisingly unstable ground. The mature Graham, with quieter energy, still consistently keeps language on its toes.

'How Are the Children Robin', (originally from Graham's 1977 collection, *Implements in their Places* and included in the *New Collected Poems*) is not one of his typical epistolary poems. A finished, lyric performance, it offers no intimation of shared subtext as, for instance, do his 'Lines on Roger Hilton's Watch', where mysteriously 'terrible times' connect poet and painter. Graham and his dedicatee, the Canadian poet Robin Skelton, seem bound more publicly, by the familiar experience of parents when a child, perhaps the last child, leaves home.

Perhaps the children could also symbolise the poets' poems, or their books.

In reading the poem aloud, Graham makes a considerable pause after uttering the first line, as if 'how are' were part of an unfinished question, and not about the children of the next line. On the page, though, the unpunctuated sentence allows further interpretations, with a hinted distress, as if there were an element of asking not only 'how did they' leave home 'so early', but 'how could they?'. The bird metaphor is set in place, without recourse to any clichés about empty nests, but with a tangible evocation of the process of 'flying leaving home'. Those double participles are echoed later in the stanza, with 'walking hoping'. All is controlled flux.

The way the speaker pricks the grandeur of his self-description as 'the poet' with the qualifier, 'I mean me', contributes to an undertone of gruff charm. This is a portrait of the poet as a father, one sharing emotions with another father. Graham is famous for the fine love-poems written to his wife Nessie (Agnes) Dunsmuir. 'How Are The Children Robin' extends the tenderness, and, without any self-consciousness or fanfare, questions conventional masculinity in advance of the 'new man' concept.

Each stanza weaves a complicated narrative (although it doesn't ever sound complicated). The act of physical walking, the entwining of memory with poetic creation and poets' conversation are among the threads. A kind of poetic trance ('the song is lost asleep') blends with the memory of singing to sleep of a child in the first stanza: there is also the arrival of spring in the blackthorn's 'white flourish'. In the second stanza, after the brilliant clarity of the remembered, scarlet-anoraked children whom, nevertheless, the speaker confesses he would never expect to see, the rhythms of the ongoing walk of a solitary figure are reasserted, beleaguered by other people and the omnipresent rain.

From the stream of consciousness of stanza 3, arises what seems to be a disjointed muttering of parental imprecations and instructions: '… let that be a lesson… / Keep off the roads'. Night falls, and the wood itself is untethered, 'flying into the dusk'. Finally, the children are imagined as birds again, though the homing may never happen. 'When shall we see the children older returning / Into the treetops? And what are they bringing?' That final enquiry seems neither frightened or suspicious, merely curious. The fluidity and compression of the poem, the impressionism and minimal punctuation, suggest a great passage of time in a small space. Almost an elegy, it is hauntingly beautiful.

www.theguardian.com/books/booksblog/2018/jan/29/ poem-of-the-week-how-are-the-children-robin-by-ws-graham

JANE YEH
Musk-Ox

His impassive side
Is an astounding wall of fur, a kind
Of dry waterfall
Formed of long strands of hair –

The unchecked growth
Of his copious wool hide
Swamps him entirely; somewhere under there
Are four unsightly legs

And hooves, but you wouldn't know it. Oversized
Powder puff – ambulatory
Moustache – through Arctic grassland
He onerously glides, his back

Festooned with jaunty tufts
Of wool. His prehistoric skull barely clears
The dense fur
Around it; a pair of drooping horns

Gamely frames
His long, sad face. If he could speak, he'd ask
For a svelter
Silhouette (or at least more

Lichens to graze on). Happiness comes
From enduring,
It seems. His tiny eyes rove over
The rich summer landscape. He lumbers

Up a crest like a minibus
Made of hair, patiently looking for
The next buffet
Of grasses. If he could choose, he'd

Be reborn
As a salmon – sleek as a torpedo
In the deep green
Water, flashing his iridescent scales.

'Musk-Ox' is from Jane Yeh's second collection, *The Ninjas*. Aingeal Clare, praising the collection in her *Guardian* review, remarked on Yeh's 'touching and exquisite animal poems, whose obvious sympathy and ready wit deserve comparisons with Marianne Moore'.

Yeh is an American poet based in London. Her voice has distinctly English as well as Amercian qualities. Combining fantasy, melancholy, precision and gently-disturbing wit, it suggests at times how Lewis Carroll could have written, had he been a young twenty-first-century postmodernist.

While Yeh often enjoys letting the various characters in her poems do the talking, her venture, in 'Musk-Ox', into third-person narration allows her a fuller focus on externals. This poem gives us the creature's impressively cumbersome, and very hairy, physical presence. At first, it's as if he were being filmed on location. Later, although we never entirely lose the more realist view of him, the poem gradually switches over from wild-life documentary to a beautiful animated cartoon, one which allows the musk-ox to morph into the identity of his dreams – that of a salmon 'In the deep green / Water, flashing his iridescent scales'.

The clustering of metaphor ('wall of fur', dry waterfall', 'oversized / Powder-puff – ambulatory / Moustache', 'a minibus / Made of hair…') suggests a technical device associated with the so-called Martian school of poets, who, in their turn, were influenced by the technique of *ostranenie* ('making strange') favoured by the Russian Formalists. Yeh, like Craig Raine in his earlier work, favours sensible-looking quatrains, cracked apart with unpredictable, sometimes jolting, line-breaks. The images are not reinforced by the rhythm but consciously disrupted by it, in a further process of defamiliarisation,

Yeh's tone is generally more overtly affectionate, though, than that of the Martian poets. For them, the love was in the close looking and detailed description. Here, there is an added, quirky characterisation. This is where the Lewis Carroll effect comes in. Yeh's musk-ox increasingly seems to become naturalised to the human world. He longs, like so many of us, for a 'svelter / Silhouette'. He absorbs our values, our judgements. The tufts of wool on his back are 'jaunty', the pair of horns 'gamely frames // His long, sad face'. This musk-ox is stoical but not entirely happy in his skin. In real life, he'd belong to a herd: in the poem, he's almost existentially alone. And so he points to a hopelessly paradoxical human desire: to meld into conformity, to shine with special beauty.

One of the pleasures of this poem, and of many other animal poems by Yeh, is the guiltless,almost jubilant acceptance of its own anthropomorphism. The stance is an honest one and sheds a two-way illumination. How can any mere human begin to relate to the (more) natural world, let alone describe it, without a degree of self-projection? No achieved poetic creature, from Christopher's Smart's cat Jeoffrey to Elizabeth Bishop's moose, is un-coloured by its human imaginer – and we should be grateful for, rather than scornful of, the vivid double-forms that express their empathy.

One day, science will confirm that most animals possess the ability to think, and that they can feel a rich range of emotions. Until then, we have the poets – and, of course, ordinary pet-owners everywhere – to remind us of our kinship with those to whom we once supposed ourselves to be the divinely-ordained superiors. Anthropomorphism need not say 'They're really just like us'; it can say, more humbly, 'We're really just like *them*'.

https://www.theguardian.com/books/booksblog/2012/dec/03/poem-of-the-week-jane-yeh

KATERINA ANGHELAKI-ROOKE

The Barber Shop

translated by Jackie Wilcox and the poet

A white rose,
the barber's towel
around your face
shining like a beetle
clinging to the petals.
Clippings scattered on the floor
were the days when I loved you so much
while the garrulous
sculptor of heads cuts away
what time had made superfluous.
Ah! That unscrupulous hand made you
even more beautiful,
the curve of your eyebrows more clearly defined
and beneath the jade of your eyes,
your flowers, your lips half opened.
The shop impressed itself on my mind
in all its detail
and little by little the nothingness
which my life would soon become
without you
came crawling
into the scented room.
You smiled in the mirror
and I crumbled
because I had you and would lose you
like life classically cut short
by a pair of ancient scissors.

It was the 'Poem of the Week' poster @ID75577 ID75577 who suggested, with good reason, that work by a contemporary Greek poet should be featured, and recommended Katerina Anghelaki-Rooke. The poster described her collection of new and selected poems in English, *The Scattered Papers of Penelope*, as 'a team work… a poetry collection filled with Katerina's talent and made with a lot of meraki'.

Anghelaki-Rooke, god-daughter of the writer Nikos Kazantzakis, was born in Athens in 1939, and is an internationally acclaimed poet and translator. Introducing her work in the current collection, the editor, Karen Van Dyck, stresses Anghelaki-Rooke's recent focus on 'gender and language'. As the title suggests, one of the strategies is to imagine the woman poet as a modern Penelope, liberating her from confinement in the original Homeric narrative but enjoying and using, in a general way, some of its symbolic opportunities: 'I wasn't weaving, I wasn't knitting / I was writing something / erasing and being erased / under the weight of the word' ('Penelope Says', tr. Karen Van Dyck). There are individual poems, prose-poems and short sequences, translated by various hands, including the editor's and the poet's own. The poster didn't specify a favourite poem so I have chosen one of mine, 'The Barber Shop', which I think fulfils the first commandment of a poem-in-translation – to open new horizons in the reader's familiar language. I hope it will appeal to new readers as a lively introduction to Anghelaki-Rooke work, and perhaps to other twentieth-century and contemporary Greek poets.

The poem begins with a startling juxtaposition of images: rose, towel, face 'shining like a beetle'. The muse is male, but heterosexuality needn't disconnect Anghelaki-Rooke from Sappho and her tradition. Technical complexity is less amenable to translation, but the 'passion' and 'observation' of the classical poet are discernible in the English version of 'The Barber Shop', suggesting a wonderful immediacy in Anghelaki-Rooke's love poems.

Once we've put together the metaphorical pieces, we see a startling trompe l'oeil: the face of the man being barbered becomes the beetle, 'clinging to the petals' of the surrounding white cloth. The picture will be developed and enriched in later lines, gradually inclining more towards realism. Meanwhile, metaphor-making continues, and the narrative enters time. Memory erases time, mixes up past and present verb-tenses. 'Clippings scattered on the floor / were the days when I loved you so much / while the garrulous / sculptor of heads cuts away / what time had made superfluous.'

The directness and simplicity of the diction, e.g. the intensifier in 'loved you so much', allows a 'spoken' emotional authority to ground the classical allusions and inventive metaphor-making. The poem is of course retrospective, not a love-letter but a voicing of unassuaged regret. The addressee is encountered, tragically, at the beginning of an inevitable loss, the visionary moment after which 'nothingness... / came crawling / into the scented room'. An impassioned personal voice is essential, and the translators capture it. That fusion of registers ('nothingness... / came crawling') is exemplary.

In the future predicted by the speaker, the 'garrulous sculptor of heads' (a description of which encapsulates the barber's vocational grandeur and his utter ordinariness) becomes a kind of male Atropos, severing the metaphorical thread of the speaker's life. As the Wikipedia entry reminds us, in Plato's *Republic* 'the three Moirai sing in unison with the music of the Seirenes. Lachesis sings the things that were, Clotho the things that are, and Atropos the things that are to be.' It seems that the song of the Fates has been quietly chanted throughout this poem.

https://www.theguardian.com/books/booksblog/2018/sep/17/poem-of-the-week-the-barber-shop-by-katerina-anghelaki-rooke

PAUL HENRY

The Black Guitar

Clearing out ten years from a wardrobe
I opened its lid and saw *Joe*
written twice in its dust, in a child's hand,
then a squiggled seagull or two.

                                        Joe, Joe
a man's tears are worth nothing,
but a child's name in the dust, or in the sand
of a darkening beach, that's a life's work.

I touched two strings, to hear how much
two lives can slip out of tune

                                        then I left it,
brought down the night on it, for fear, Joe
of hearing your unbroken voice, or the sea
if I played it.

The late U.A. Fanthorpe said an interesting thing – about poetry and about Paul Henry – when she described the latter as someone who 'gets the maximum effect from minimum language'. Her words are quoted on the back of his recent New and Selected Poems, *The Brittle Sea,* as well as those of Sheenagh Pugh, referring to Henry's 'musicality, his use of back-story and his ability to create the most haunting resonance'. These descriptions point to the reasons why Henry's poems are such a pleasure to read and hear. Henry is not a minimalist poet, exactly, but there is often a beautiful economy to his writing.

'The Black Guitar', originally published in his fifth collection, *Ingrid's Husband* (Seren, 2007), is a sonnet, one of the more impressionistic of its kind. It includes lines that are barely lines – phrases on the edge of silence. Two of these fragmentary lines are set to the right of the text, reminders, perhaps, of the bilateral art of the musician.

To begin with, the territory feels fairly solid and familiar. The wardrobe-clearing might be the start of a comfortable little narrative journey into a gently poignant past. But the wardrobe conceals a further, more unsettling set of memories. The guitar is not named in the body of the poem, except in terms of the pronoun, 'its' in the first quatrain and 'it' in the last. There is no detailed description. The reader's eye instead is directed to the name, 'Joe', and the 'squiggled seagull or two'.

We meet the name Joe in italics in line 2. Then it breaks the silence of the 5th line, occurring twice, so we can imagine the childish letters picked out in pale dust on the instrument's black wooden surface. But 'Joe, Joe' is not only a visual device: it's the beginning of an address to the child. The emotion builds.

In the next three lines the intensity comes from the moral re-focusing, the dismissal of 'a man's tears' beside the 'life's work' of a child's name, written in dust and, on another occasion, in sand. The term, 'life's work', ordinary enough but made striking by its context, encloses an immeasurable set of processes – the life-work of conception, birth, growth. How much has to happen mentally and physically for a child to learn to write his name? And how much for a life to make its mark in a world of dust and darkening?

The guitar, being dusty, must have already fallen into disuse when the boy wrote his inscription. Perhaps this is why the emotion is so painful. Before the solitary father unearthed the guitar, a solitary child performed the same action, signing an ownership and connection that perhaps felt tenuous.

'Two' is the essential number in the poem. It evokes separated lives, as well as the two hands that play music. That the name is written twice suggests the doubled identity one name might contain. In the ninth line, the phrase 'two strings' introduces the idea of disharmony. Being out of tune, the strings' relationship with each other is distorted.

The few end-rhymes are delicate and unforced. Particularly effective is the internal rhyme of 'touched… much' in line 9, like a tentative plucking of the strings.

The final repetition of the child's name in line 12 marks a calming-down, a turn into a more conversational register. The poem's forestalled climax, however, is the reference to the sea and the child's voice, memories which would be brought to life if the speaker played the instrument. A resonance so painful has to be deferred. There's relief when the memories and their sounds are shut away, un-summoned.

I find the whole poem strangely mimetic, as if the sonnet itself had mysteriously turned into the guitar. Its sound-box is left vibrating with emotional chords that, once touched, linger a long time in the reader's mind.

https://www.theguardian.com/books/booksblog/2010/nov/08/ poem-of-the-week-paul-henry

CLIFF FORSHAW

Loop

62 seconds of the extinct Thylacine or Tasmanian Tiger on film.

Within the box, it growls, it twists,
scowls through its repertoire of tricks,
ignores the camera – or gurns up close, turns
again, to flop, to gnaw that paw-trapped bone.

It paces out its trap of light; one hundred reps
while hindquarters zither bars of sun;
claws cage's mesh, hangs stretched
as if to take the measure of itself.

You saw. You see. And what we've got is what was shot:
short clips, fragments caught and stitched
together in a loop of black and white.

Nine lives? Not quite. It's down. It's out.
It's on its feet and born again. Like a repetition
compulsion, like… like reincarnated light.

‘Loop’ is the opening sonnet of a chapbook-length sequence, *Tiger*. Forshaw’s subject is the Tasmanian tiger, more properly known as the thylacine (from Thylacinus Cynocephalus, ‘the dog-headed pouched one’). Also known as the Tasmanian wolf, it was an extraordinary creature – not a tiger, not a wolf, but a golden-brown marsupial dog with tiger-like black stripes. It was able to move on two feet as well as four, and both genders had a pouch. In the case of the male, the pouch protected the scrotal sac from damage when the animal moved through deep undergrowth. Despite such useful design features, the thylacine became virtually extinct in Australia and New Guinea around 2,000 years ago.

The last thylacines found refuge in Tasmania, then they, too, disappeared, their widespread slaughter encouraged by bounties. The species was declared extinct in 1986. Nonetheless, there have been many reported sightings since, resulting in a campaign for its re-classification as rare and endangered. Meanwhile, the thylacine survives as Tasmania’s national emblem and favourite icon: ‘Extinct, this creature’s everywhere / from CD sleeves to bottled beer’ as another poem, ‘Barcode’, puts it.

The poems in *Tiger* are sometimes elegiac, but more often jaunty, ironic snapshots that reveal the antics of homo sapiens in relation to the animal world. Their concern is with unvarnished actuality. The poet examines the thylacine as museum exhibit, and records recent desperate attempt at extracting the DNA from a preserved foetus so as to reconstitute the animal by cloning. The comically sad fact that so much has been done for the thylacine far too late in the day emerges to reinforce the title of the sequence, *Tiger*, as a reminder of another species currently in particularly urgent need of protection.

‘Loop’ revisits the film of a captive thylacine made by the naturalist David Fleay in 1933. Fleay was in pursuit of live animals, and his traps were humane, but the last line of the first stanza of 'Loop' reminds us of the miserable deaths thylacines usually suffered at the hands of casual trappers. Later, the image of the living but captive animal coalesces with that of a creature killed and displayed as a trophy, hanging 'stretched / as if to take the measure of itself'.

Even in the poem, the thylacine is elusive. Continually pacing, it ignores the camera or 'gurns up close'. The abortive movement of the caged animal is caught in the compression of a number of internal rhymes: 'growls' / 'scowls', 'gurns' / 'turns'. The end-rhymes are assonantal, mostly, with only one full rhyme: 'white' / 'light'. The hardest-hitting rhymes occur on the first line of the sestet, reinforced by the caesurae. 'You saw. You see. And what we've got is what was shot' leaves us in no doubt as to the double-meaning of 'shot'. The variability of the rhymes, and the push-pull effect of lines whose regularity is never guaranteed, help to reinforce a sense of tough vitality stringently checked.

The poem begins with a physical box, suggesting both the cage and the camera. And it summons further metaphorical cages devised in the effort to preserve or mimic life. The film itself becomes a 'trap of light'. The technique of stitching together 'short clips' to make a continuous loop connects film to poetry, and perhaps the sonnet in particular, a form emphatic in its sections. From island to zoo to film to sonnet, the thylacine seems to move into ever-narrowing enclosure.

The poem juxtaposes the finality of the creature's extinction with the immortality traditionally conferred by art. 'It's down. It's out' but at the same time 'It's on its feet and born again'. The analogy with obsessive compulsive behaviour ('repetition compulsion') might go beyond cinematic technique to suggest not only the animal's trapped pacing, but the pattern-making instinct of the artist. A final irony is that celluloid film, the very medium of 'reincarnated light' which still give grainy life to the thylacine, is now itself a nearly extinct technology.

https://www.theguardian.com/books/2011/nov/22/poem-of-the-week-cliff-forshaw

BILLY MILLS
Tiny Pieces

scattered
this glass
reconstitutes

folds
determine

*

follow
the lines

come
again

*

sun
after rain

luminous
leaves

boxroom
window

*

various greens

a pair of thrushes

*

first
the world

next
the word

imperfect
charting

*

close
now

slowly
come

*

touch
call
remember

simple
pleasures

*

here
where

all
is

tiny
pieces

The *Collected Poems* where 'Tiny Pieces' originates is titled *Lares/Manes,* but concern with hearth and home is only part of the story. The vast and flowing home of the poems belongs to geological time.

Billy Mills's approach is not confined to asking questions about language. His work combines the musicality and intensity of poetry with the precision of scientific method, and the collection has the intellectual capaciousness of the bigger literary forms: it contains data of all kinds, found poetry, philosophical enquiry, and a variety of landscapes and cityscapes. While Mills is associated with a group of experimental Irish poets claiming independence from the traditional emphasis on identity politics, his poetry is fully alive to location. The fact that it doesn't sing rhetorically about Ireland doesn't mean that Ireland is excluded from the 'important places' it considers.

A poem in sections, 'Tiny Pieces' forms part of a larger work, 'What is a Mountain?' There is a trio of epigraphs: a brief report on the three car-bombs detonated in the centre of Dublin with the likely connivance of British Army intelligence, a quotation from Oscar Wilde ('All art is entirely useless') and a verse by Godfraidh Fionn O Daláigh, 'If they ask questions / *skilful poets will know; / bright this art you hear of: / questions the door to knowing.'*

The imagery of mountain-formation is introduced in a further, untitled prelude. 'What is a mountain?' asks the 5th line. 'Stone flows; folds. A name. It rises.' In the miniature-scale delicacy of the 'Tiny Pieces' which follow, we find the inverse of the mountain and its associated cataclysm. What gradually emerges (each tiny piece has its own page in the collection) is tenderly consoling – a love poem more intimate and more spacious than such poems usually are.

The first section considers both fragmentation ('scattered / this glass') and reintegration. 'Folds' is a key word which will later give rise to three poems described as folds ('The First Fold', etc.) Fold mountains are formed by the collision of two tectonic plates, and the compressed material both rises and descends. 'Folds' in the earth's crust 'determine' the shape of a mountain. 'Folds' as sheltering-places also form our allegiances, and thus our blind-spots and our wars. Paper and poems are folded into shapes: lovers enfold one another. As the second poem suggests, tact and precision might inform and transform relations. With 'Follow the lines' we move from particulate and scattered to particular and enclosing.

The imagistic third section seems to excavate memory. Vividly present, the shining leaves (more tiny pieces) somehow lead back as well as up to the 'boxroom / window'. 'Window' reconstitutes the scattered glass. The images suggest to me a child's room, looking down on a small garden fronted with privet: safe containment, but with a view outwards. The symmetrical syllable-count 1/3/3/1/2/2 gives this poem the balance of a miniature sonnet.

The next segment stays with the natural world: it's the most haiku-like of the pieces, and the depth of the stanza break seems to stand for the 'cutting word' – often not a word, but a punctuation mark heightening the significance of a juxtaposition. Here, the thrushes emerge from the 'various greens' and the printless space with the magical suddenness of actual birds seen suddenly close up, and with all the potential offered by 'a pair'.

Perhaps the thrushes help attune the reader to the sense of new young life, which is implicit in the next piece. The rift between the world and the word, the 'imperfect charting', after all begins with our earliest speech. Aligning word and world as accurately as possible is our first and life-long human concern.

Exactness of language can at least find out the question and glimpse 'the door to knowing'. In the 6th poem it finds song. This four-word invitation is a perfect musical phrase: 'close / now // slowly / come'. Its unexpected, Latinate syntax, culminating in the verb, takes us from word to word, pause to pause. Having once read the sentence in this initially curious structure, it becomes impossible to imagine it otherwise.

The lines in 'Tiny Pieces' are themselves tiny. I counted 30 single-word lines out of 38, half of which are monosyllables: the longest line is 'a pair of thrushes'. But it's this brevity which helps focus attention. The tempo, in music, would be adagio. Words assert their primary meanings, but the silence around them allows us to hear other tones and resonance. So in the next poem, the simple verbs (perhaps imperatives) give the reader memory-room. We're guided, told that the verbs represent 'simple pleasures', but the exact associations of 'touch', 'call' and 'remember' are gifts for private unwrapping.

By the end of the poem, the shimmer of scattered glass is distant. The last segment might complete the sentence of the previous one: 'here / where // all / is // tiny / pieces' could denote the intimate space of a body or a room, the words of the poem itself, or the molecular structure of all matter. It could denote all these things simultaneously. And still the poem has a lightness and brightness with its images of leaves and building birds, its careful looking and touching. This sense of abundance and flourishing will continue throughout 'What is a Mountain?'

https://www.theguardian.com/books/2011/nov/07/poem-of-the-week-billy-mills

ANDREW LAMBETH

Why the swan

Because the swan floats
up close.

Because the swan has no life
off past the cut-off.

Because the swan is a knife
turned in on itself.

Because the swan erases
unwhite surfaces.

Because the swan is a sign of
what to expect, like a specked cough.

Because the swan isn't
drawn like an ear. It listens

but it won't hear, won't look
up in time. It's as if it's stuck.

Because the air shushes sirens,
because the canal divulges silence,

because the curves have been stolen
from what's left of the swan,

which is its song, of course –
the long stretch between locks.

The author of this poem will be known to many 'Poem of the Week' readers as the enigmatically-named poster, nosuchzone. Largely spared a formal education, and entirely innocent of the university Eng. Lit. or Creative Writing qualification, Andrew Lambeth is a typographer. He edits the Leeds-based literary journal, *Strix*, and is still comparatively new to writing poetry. Publication is not a priority for him, but it's still good to see that his work is beginning to be more widely recognised. Recently, for example, he was published by Helen Mort and Stuart Maconie in their anthology of pub-related poetry, *One for the Road*.

It's surprising, at first glance, to find him writing about a swan. Swans, after all, are the most literary of birds. A substantial and high-quality swan-poem anthology (proposed title, *Swan Songs,* of course) would begin with Orlando Gibbons and welcome into its pages, among others, W.B. Yeats, Sara Teasdale, Stevie Smith. Baudelaire with his almost unbearably tragic 'Le Cygne', and, of course, Judith Willson (see page 31). These poetic swans are variously symbolic: in Teasdale's verses, for example, they are a silent chorus, an unspoken erotic commentary, intensifying the lovers' gaze on one another. Swans aren't always associated with grief and death, an association borne of the once widely-held but baseless notion that they sing only when about to die. The Greek legend, in which Apollo's soul becomes a swan, may be more significant; write about a swan, and you're inevitably writing about high art. Whatever they symbolise, poetry's swans are rarely just swans. Even in real birdlife, a swan is a powerful, ambivalent presence, both coarse and ethereal, with a neck like a weaponised question-mark.

Lambeth's title, 'Why the swan', could be interpreted as a question, possibly about the swan's status as poetic material, with the ensuing couplets (all of which, apart from the last, start with 'Because') forming a list of unpredictable answers.

The poem may want to explain each time, 'this is why swans are supercharged visual and literary emblems' and perhaps, also, explain why they shouldn't be so stereotyped. But it also seems, at least sometimes, that the poem is asking plaintively why *this particular swan* has been singled out, not for poetry, but for abuse. Early on, the truncated-seeming lines, with their unexpected breaks and unsettling para-rhyme, intimate mortality: 'the swan has no life / off past the cut-off', '(it) is a knife / turned in on itself'. Stanza 4 glances aside, in homage to immaculate whiteness. But the death-resonance sounds increasingly as the poem develops. The swan itself becomes an ominous sign, 'like a specked cough' (note the spitty alliteration of 'expect' and 'specked'). It's hard at this point not to think of the terminally-sick, expectorating Keats. The figure of the tubercular poet, like the swan, attracts false romanticism.

Readers of Strix will have the advantage of comparing 'Why the swan' with the neighbouring poem, 'Towpath (tinnitus)'. The latter, earthier and more subjective, focuses on a 'strange singing' which wrests the poet's descriptive powers into inventive analogy. The sound is 'Like singing / backwards. Like whistling inside croaking –' and later becomes 'a whistle stretched / to a fine scream'. There's no swan on the canal in this poem, although other birds are noted, but perhaps it's the un-nerving, unidentifiable (and possibly internally produced) singing heard in 'Towpath (tinnitus)' which forms the background music, and some of the impetus, of 'Why the swan'.

The poet's visually trained eye brilliantly connects the bird's shape with listening and hearing. When the swan sleeps, with its head buried in the feathers of its back, the outline resembles that of a large ear. But the resemblance involves simultaneous denial. This particular swan or its image 'isn't / drawn like an ear', a statement underlining the bird's essential distance from the human species, and possibly the pathos of super-human sensory awareness combined with the inability to interpret the noise of threat.

Off-stage, out of the picture, some seeming drama occurs: 'It… won't look up in time. It's as if it's stuck.' Stanzas 8 and 9 begin with the ominous noise of sirens and their 'shushing' and silencing by collusive air, and end with the drab rawness of 'what's left of the swan'.

The final couplet defines 'what's left' not as physical remains, but as 'song'. This isn't a comfortingly aesthetic return to tradition: the song is equated with something mundane and industrial, 'the long stretch between locks'. That 'long stretch' may consist of the canal's water, the tow-path, or life itself; the 'locks' may be the kind which enable passage, or frustrate it. The phrase reminds us of the Orlando Gibbons lyrics, in which death has 'unlocked' the swan's throat. Inevitably, 'stretched' suggests Baudelaire's caged swan, escaped and lost in a Parisian street, desperately straining its neck towards the sky. Lambeth's swan earns an honourable place in the later pages of that swan-anthology, the bird's latest incarnation as a flawed, elusive emblem appropriate to the place and time.

'Why the swan' is one of the two poems by Andrew Lambeth published in Issue 5 of *Strix*. Ian Harker was the acting editor for this issue.

https://www.theguardian.com/books/booksblog/2019/jan/14/
poem-of-the-week-why-the-swan-by-andrew-lambeth

PHILIP FRIED

Yoga for Leaders and Others

Mountain Pose

Stand tall, with feet together,
shoulders relaxed. Emote
the imperturbable power
of mountains to endure
pelting rain and rockfall,
erosion's perpetual terror.
Indignation is elemental
but the peak does not acknowledge
the collateral damage of scree.

Take three deep breaths, resume
holiday, stay in touch.

Warrior Pose

Stand with legs apart
like sturdy tree roots, right
foot turned out 90 degrees
and left foot turned in slightly.
With right hand seize the horizon
and stare out, emanating
an aura of sensitive menace
that says while the day will be won
the losses are personally felt.

Hold for one minute before
resuming normal posture.

Bridge Pose

Like a bridge over turbulent water,
lie supine on floor with knees
bent. Place arms at sides,
exhale, then press downward and lift
hips. Bringing chest toward chin –
your whole body enacting
the need to be calm, in the face
of probable injustice –
hold for just one minute.

Model a deep breath
and resume holiday.

Child's Pose

Like a villager, squat on your heels.
Roll your torso forward,
bringing your forehead to rest
on the bed in front of you
letting your body express
its grief of gristle and bone.
Lower your chest as close
to your knees as you comfortably can.
All viewers will understand.

No need to speak. Hold
the pose and breathe. Just breathe.

In the trenchantly political poems of Philip Fried's collection, *Squaring the Circle*, reviewer Jonathan Timbers heard overtones of W.H. Auden. Fried, an American poet working in a global context every bit as murky as Auden's *'low dishonest decade'* is differently, perhaps more democratically, bold. The gently scolding Auden tone – perhaps best described as materteral or simply auntie-ish – is absent and might be missed by fans of 'the English Auden'. The poets' cultural contexts are very different. But Fried's forthright insistence on the ethical responsibility of poetry links him with Auden's moral tradition. Neither political in the subtle avant garde manner, nor a 'spoken word' ranter, Fried is a word-smith with a public shit-detector, and a lively ear for the new vernacular. He understands precisely the ways language has learned to lie.

The geometer's (impossible) challenge of squaring the circle has form as a metaphor. Fried's collection extends it in various ways, including the corporeal. In the 'Poem of the Week' sequence, it's the human body which occupies space through the more flexible geometric figures of Yoga. All the poems describe actual poses, while they themselves pose as how-to guides for 'the leaders and others' to square their circles, demonstrate fake emotions or flaunt responsibilities they have evaded.

It's almost as if the poems were instructions on how to turn into a statue. Each reinforces this sense of 3D solidity by a rectangular-looking 9-line stanza, seemingly erected on the plinth of a more insistently imperative couplet. The figures seem poised between sculptural image and live body preparing for the photo-shoot or video camera. Such ambiguity makes a good analogy for the conflicts and subterfuge of personal empire-building. Fried may hope to set up, by means of contrast, the qualities which might make a bad leader good. However, his main focus is on the dubious art of 'appearances' and how the bad leader might 'model' a stance of power and virtue, although everyone, leader included, knows the stance to be fake.

The first three poses evoke a clearly perceived opposition, a populace, critical and unhappy, which presents a threat to the leadership. The stance advised is constructed as much by that domestic threat as by a statement of achievement. In *Mountain Pose*, power is the bare peak which rears above the weather, well able to withstand it and allow for 'the collateral damage of scree'. The instructor's tone is almost mocking: the contrived, second-hand diction acknowledges the flakiness of the pose. 'Emote / the imperturbable power / of mountains to endure [...]', the instructor says, and goes on to give the game away: 'Take three deep breaths, / resume / holiday, stay in touch.' The leader isn't even at work!

Suspense is established, even before the first poem: who doesn't hope that pride will go before a fall? Moral outrage almost gets its wish in *Warrior Pose*, where the Leader is made to look awkwardly theatrical, almost ready to trip over that in-turned left foot. The oxymnoron 'sensitive menace' reminds us of the intricately nuanced distortion leadership requires. The leader isn't allowed to show his/her full pugnacity on camera. There must be a veneer of empathy even as the horizon itself is seized (the moment when I first began to think God might be one of the 'others' requiring instruction).

If the imaginary leader is not quite Auden's totalitarian Ogre, plenty of aspirant despots fill his place, some nearer home than is comfortable. And yet the poem isn't simply about the abuses of power. It includes 'poses' which might be genuine, useful, humane, although impossible to sustain. *The Bridge* offers images of self-sacrifice, although these are undermined in the couplet's advice to 'Model a deep breath / and resume holiday'.

Still, we seem to be getting nearer to an idea of how power might redeem itself, and *Child's Pose* is its culmination.

Now it's made clear that the leader is being televised: 'All viewers will understand'. The prostration the move requires (and the title) somehow suggests A.A. Milne's Christopher Robin, praying 'at the foot of the bed'. But in Fried's poem, the adult body is being trusted with an expression of fallibility, 'its grief of gristle and bone'. The final injunction to 'Hold / the pose and breathe. Just breathe' is significant. At last the instructor has abandoned irony. There's a certain hope that the body's rediscovered naturalness and simplicity might engender a rediscovered humanity, and the reconciliation of the leaders with those 'others' who are led.

https://www.theguardian.com/books/booksblog/2017/nov/20/ poem-of-the-week-yoga-for-leaders-and-others-by-philip-fried

ROBYN BOLAM

Moving On

In the Haymarket a bus station has been transformed
from cattle crush to airport lounge. I no longer miss
Marlborough Crescent, open to weather. From there, I'd rush
for the trolley bus to school while the abattoir let
blood flow unchecked along the gutter, stinking through fumes
as drivers climbed in their cabs and, one by one, engines
vibrated, buses pulled into stands. I'd leap across,
never connecting that red stream with the death it meant
or managing to link this to cattle sometimes glimpsed.
Our city made blood, tanks and ships. It still stood on coal.

Near to where we waited in the cold, suits with laptops
raise glasses in the lobby of a high-rise hotel.
Phones vibrate silently; clean shoes press the shining floor.
Automatic doors open, close by a subdued road.
Multi-glazed rooms gaze across the river. It must be
better; no more leading to slaughter. Downstream they dredged
the Tyne at Wallsend for the deepest vessel ever
to sail there –fifty feet of it underwater – so
they could load the last remains of shipbuilding up
for Dahbol. Blood down the gutter: water under the bridge.

The author of 'Moving On', Robyn Bolam, is originally from the Tyne Valley, Northumberland. Newcastle upon Tyne isn't the only location her poetry maps as it explores its central theme of 'roots' but it remains an important home, or 'hyem', and is one of those sources re-visited and re-envisioned in her eponymous recent collection. What I like about the current poem, and others in *Hyem*, is the detached observation which laces the commemorative affection, and keeps the genre's nostalgic tendency under control.

It's a quality of balance that underlies the tangible, physical, archaeological layering in 'Moving On'. The city of the 1960s and its twenty-first century transformation are fused in a single imaginative space, in which two speakers, the schoolgirl and the adult, assert different points of view.

The bus-station has relocated to the Haymarket from Marlborough Crescent, and the new 'airport lounge' replaces the remembered 'cattle crush', but memory impinges on current perception via a mental process familiar to most adults but no less fascinating and complex. Do we ever fully see the new thing if its early image is already deeply engrained in our younger minds? Such double-exposures are often, of course, poetic homeland.

The speaker, while remembering, appears to respond to contemporary pressures, in which 'the market' and personal development may collude, towards 'moving on'. The superior comforts and shininess of the new are duly appreciated. They're also registered as having less emotional weight than the industrial-imperial past. Neither old or new is thoughtlessly romanticised. The poem seems founded on an honest act of reportage, in which emotion is, deliberately muted. It avoids antithesis, the luxury of showing irreconcilably violent contrast.

The new phase of post-industrial development seems to extinguish the past with the sensory force of absolute reality, but the poet senses connections. One of them is carried in the idea of vibration. In the first stanza, the vibration is tangible and audible: '… one by one, engines / vibrated, buses pulled into stands'. In the second, 'phones vibrate silently', as if the mechanisation represented by the internal combustion engine had continued to advance, but become sleek and subterranean. Scepticism, hinted by the ironical title, emerges clearly in the summing-up, and that resisting, jolting rhythm of 'It must be / better; no more leading to slaughter'.

Innocence and ignorance are gently interrogated by raised consciousness. The speaker's young self would thoughtlessly 'leap across' the blood-filled gutter, unable to connect it with the butchery of the abattoir and the glimpsed cattle. Blood has seemed to the child simply another product. 'Our city made blood, tanks and ships. It still stood on coal.' Two voices I think speak either side of that caesura, one the child's, the second, the adult's, for whom time's passing registers in the 'still' which implies 'though not anymore'.

Again, there is continuity as well as revision. The adult speaker understands the source of the blood and has therefore learned from the child to suspect the apparently clean, glassy renovations. Though political criticism is covert, it's present as irony. The poem knows that the 'leading to slaughter' carries on, and metaphorical blood may be spilled under euphemisms of progress, 'suits' words like redundancy, restructuring and sustainability. Shit becomes bull-shit in the corporate city, and locating it, understanding its cause and opposing it remain almost impossible for the individual kept perpetually moving by the city's many wheels.

The two halves of the poem form a visual representation of division-plus-parity, with the final, laconically sad images ('Blood down the gutter: water under the bridge') carrying the past and its images inexorably away, but retaining the inference of cruel and unfinished decimation. The Tyne at Wallsend, we learn from a significantly timed after-thought, has yielded up the remains of the 'deepest vessel ever to sail there' (the Osprey, I think?) for final despatch to India. The devastation of the region's shipbuilding industry (the poet Tom Pickard being one of its finest documenters) is registered, inevitably and fairly, as traumatic loss. But 'Moving On' is also a blending of two cities and eras into a more nuanced space where the walker/reader can cross bridges, retrace steps, pause, and question how deep the differences really lie.

Poems by Robyn Bolam, including Moving On, feature in *The Land of Three Rivers*, Neil Astley's anthology of verse from, and about, the North East of England. I should 'declare an interest', having a short poem of my own included, but add that 'Moving On', like all 'Poems of the Week', tapped *me* on the shoulder first; I picked it after I'd finished *Hyem* and before I'd opened the anthology. Both *Hyem* and *The Land of Three Rivers* are belta (Geordie, 'really good'). Trust me, even if I'm a southerner.

https://www.theguardian.com/books/booksblog/2018/jan/15/poem-of-the-week-moving-on-by-robyn-bolam

MARILYN HACKER

A Braid of Garlic

Aging women mourn while they go to market,
buy fish, figs, tomatoes, enough *today* to
feed the wolf asleep underneath the table
who wakes from what dream?

What but loss comes round with the changing season?
He is dead, whom, daring, I called a brother
with that leftover life perched on his shoulder
cawing departure.

He made one last roll of the dice. He met his
last, best interlocutor days before he
lay down for the surgery that might/might not
extend the gamble.

What they said belongs to them. Now a son writes
elegies, though he has a living father.
One loves sage tea, one gave the world the scent of
his mother's coffee.

Light has shrunk back to what it was in April,
incrementally will shrink back to winter.
I can't call my peregrinations 'exile,'
but count the mornings.

In a basket hung from the wall, its handle
festooned with cloth flowers from chocolate boxes,
mottled purple shallots, and looped beside it,
a braid of garlic.

I remember, ten days after a birthday
(counterpoint and candlelight in the wine-glass),
how the woman radiologist's fingers
probed, not caressing.

So, reprise (what wasn't called a 'recurrence')
of a fifteen-years-ago rite of passage:
I arrived, encumbered with excess baggage,
scarred, on the threshold.

Through the mild winter sun in February,
two or three times weekly to Gobelins, the
geriatric hospital where my friend was
getting her nerve back.

At the end of elegant proofs and lyric,
incoherent furious trolls in diapers.
Fragile and ephemeral as all beauty:
the human spirit –

while the former journalist watched, took notes and
shocked, regaled her visitors with dispatches
from the war zone in which she was embedded,
biding her time there.

Now in our own leftover lives, we toast our
memories and continence. I have scars where
breasts were, her gnarled fingers, these days, can hardly
hold the pen steady.

Thousands mourn him, while in the hush and hum of
life-support for multiple organ failure,
utter solitude, poise of scarlet wings that
flutter, and vanish.

'A Braid of Garlic' comes originally from Marilyn Hacker's 2010 collection, *Names*. As suggested by the title, and the dedication the book carries, 'In Memory of Hayden Carruth, Mahmoud Darwish and Reginald Shepherd', many presences and literary mentors are invoked. These guardian spirits, living and dead, local and distant, have their appropriate modes of address. Among the verse-letters are less familiar forms. A favourite form of Hacker's is the *glosa*, in which lines from another writer's work are woven into a new poem, and, for her conversations with Arabic writers, the now thoroughly westernised form, the *ghazal*.

'A Braid of Garlic', the last poem in the collection, is partly an elegy for Darwish 'whom, daring, I called a brother'. The verse is written in an informal Sapphic quatrain, its stanzas sometimes impressionistic 'scenes' or vivid jottings. The 'dying fall' of the feminine endings and foreshortened last lines seems appropriate to the overall mood. But against this sorrowful cadence is pitted a vigorous appetite for joy and survival, expressed in the muscularity of the syntax, and embodied by the 'aging women' who continue valiantly to shop and write and celebrate their 'memories and continence'.

That little litany of fruit and vegetables in the poem's second line is the opening gambit against the 'loss' that 'comes round with every changing season'. Alertness to every-day sensuous pleasures underlines one of the affinities with Darwish. The speaker is observing what is surely a Parisian market, and savouring its smells and colours. Stanza 6 is like a still-life, with its decorated, homely basket of 'mottled purple shallots' and the garlic-braid looped nearby. The images spark off memories, the 'counterpoint and candle-light' of a birthday celebration followed by an unsettling medical diagnosis. The braid of sensory experience is a life-line and a bridge, but there is always a 'wolf asleep underneath the table'. A seasonal reversal unsettles the narrative: the full summer light seems to fade, dwindling first to April (stanza 5) and then to February's 'mild winter sun' (stanza 9). Writing, like living, means taking chances. Preparing for the life-or-death risk of surgery, Darwish wrote, 'this poem is a dice throw / onto a board of darkness / that glows and doesn't glow / words fall / like feathers on sand' ('The Dice Player'). Hacker's poems aren't feathery or provisional: they are packed and dense, but also active, full of movement and shifts of perspective. This one turns outwards again towards the heroism of another woman writer struggling after ill health to 'get her nerve back'. The 'elegant proofs and lyric' and the 'incoherent furious trolls in diapers' make a memorable antithesis. This is endurable, the poem seems to say, only because both exist on the same continuum – he 'human spirit'.

Finally the poem returns to Darwish, and his last moments. The butterfly, one of his significant images, symbolises the soul, of course, but it becomes a metaphor here for physical reality: we see the colour of surgery, 'crimson', and the 'wings' seem like an opened chest-cavity, exposing the faltering heart.

Garlic, old folk-cure for numerous ills and device against vampires, can't stop the butterfly from vanishing. But the braided stanzas of a poem are tenacious, forming a tough loop of imagination and language that might outlast death. Whether the writer's war-zone is a country, or her body, or both, this poem reminds us, as does the poetry of Darwish, that the demand is essentially the same: to bear witness.

https://www.theguardian.com/books/booksblog/2010/may/10/poem-week-braid-of-garlic

JOHN KINSELLA

Chainsaw

The seared flesh of wood, cut
to a polish, deceives: the rip and tear
of the chain, its rapid cycling
a covering up of raw savagery.
It is not just machine. In the blur
of its action, in its guttural roar,
it hides the malice of organics.
Cybernetic, empirical, absolutist.
The separation of Church and state,
conspiracies against the environmental
lobby, enforcement of fear, are at the core
of its modus operandi. The cut of softwood
is deceptive, hardwood dramatic: just
before dark on a chill evening
the sparks rains out – dirty wood,
hollowed by termites, their digested
sand deposits, capillaried highways
imploded: the chainsaw effect.
It is not subtle. It is not ambient.
It is trans nothing. A clogged airfilter
has it sucking up more juice –
it gargles, floods, chokes
into silence. Sawdust dresses boots,
jeans, the field. Gradually
the paddock is cleared, the wood
stacked in cords along the lounge-room wall.
A darkness kicks back and the cutout
bar jerks into place, a distant chainsaw
dissipates. Further on, some seconds later,
another does the same. They follow

the onset of darkness, a relay of severing,
a ragged harmonics stretching back
to its beginning – gung-ho,
blazon, overconfident. Hubristic
to the final cut, last drop of fuel.

In the wheatlands of John Kinsella's Western Australia, cultivation equals war. Perhaps it does everywhere: it merely looks like a kindlier exchange where climates are more hospitable.

'Chainsaw', which first appeared in *New Poems:Peripheral Light* (2003), takes us uncomfortably close to one of the weapons, showing us the way it sounds and works and the kind of wounds it inflicts. Relatively short lines, three or four-stressed, with no stanza-breaks, produce an almost tree-like, vertical visual structure: the lines, often enjambed, sometimes staccato, fluid but given to grainy stops and starts, suggest the hidden intricacies of the tree and the incursions of the saw. There may be more metaphorical 'kickback' here than is first apparent. Versification is traditionally compared to ploughing, with good etymological reason, but perhaps the motion of the chainsaw is equally indicative.

The poem begins by warning us to look beyond the cut wood's smooth, polished-looking surface to 'the rip and tear / of the chain, its rapid cycling / a covering up of raw savagery'. The savagery is expanded and politically contexutualised in the ensuing lines. It ranges from the 'malice of organics' to the anti-environmental 'conspiracies' of agribusiness. Why is 'separation of Church and State' included in the trinity of evils? Perhaps it's a metaphor denoting the schizophrenia inherent in civilisation's compartmentalisation, as applied to humans and their environment. 'Organics' may suggest pesticides, fertilisers, etc. based on vegetable or animal compounds: at the same time it invoke the word's Greek origins – *organikos,* meaning machine or instrument. The pun on 'cycling' (the chain of the chainsaw literally recycles itself, and destroys the cycle-chain's innocence) is a further example of the depth to the cuts Kinsella makes with his word-choice.

The verbal layering may involve irony: that the wood is judged 'dirty' by the human operatives is the result of its providing life-support to the termite populations. The triple-patterning could become repetitive but doesn't, perhaps because of its placing in the line and because it involves different parts of speech: 'gargles, floods, chokes', 'boots, / jeans, the field', 'gung-ho, / blazon, overconfident'. Here 'blazon' is used as an adjective, with striking effect. Finally, the chainsaws cease their activities for the night, but there is an ominous sense of their relentless tomorrows – which, of course, are humanity's tomorrows. Chainsaws are us. And we'll go on noisily masticating the earth's resources unless we power-off and listen to the complex, non-sloganeering voices like Kinsella's. Between the lines, 'Chainsaw' shows that beauty as well as politics has power. The biodiversity of the diction and rhythms packed into its small space reminds us the ecosystem we're part of is a magnificent poem in progress. Don't eat it, don't shit on it: read it.

https://www.theguardian.com/books/booksblog/2016/jan/25/ poem-of-the-week-chainsaw-by-john-kinsella

PETER BALAKIAN

World Trade Center / Mail Runner / '73

There was no languor, no drowsy trade winds,
or stoned-out stupor of lapping waves,

only news, the big board of crime,
corporate raiding, selling short and long.

It didn't matter, I was no Ishmael.
I just hovered there in the thick of the material –

at the edge of a skyline of money,
rising in a glass box.

It was comic to think Bachelard believed elevators
had destroyed the heroism of stair-climbing.

In the rush of soaring metallic, past the whiff of 4-martini lunches,
up gearless traction in transparency,

waves of cool air coming from the vents.
At the 85th in a sky lobby we stalled out and the sun

flooded the glass / the river / the cliffs.
Jersey was just gouache and platinum coming apart –
a glistening smudge

and some nagging line from Roethke I'd been reading –
circulating the air:
'It will come again. Be still. Wait.'

The opening section of Peter Balakian's collection, *Ziggurat,* alternates ekphrastic poems on artworks by Andy Warhol with recollections of the World Trade Centre and surrounding cityscape some thirty years before the devastation of 9/11. Balakian was a messenger for a Lower Manhattan shipping company, regularly delivering mail to offices in the newly erected building. The original ziggurats of the Middle East were vast structures, many of which supported a shrine, so the title has its irony: this tower is a fiscal temple. But it's not only that. Interviewed by Scott Simon, Balakian recalled the major aesthetic impact of the new architecture, and how, at the time, it opened 'mental spaces' for him.

Public icons more sombre than Warhol's soup-cans, 'Blue Jackie' and 'Electric Chair '63', flank 'World Trade Centre / Mail Runner / '73'. In another Warhol poem, the narrator is at the Whitney Museum of American Art, 'staring at the pink face of Marilyn Monroe' while able to smell 'the smouldering high-tech plastic // as it burned the air' ('Warhol / Madison Ave. / 9-11'). These disturbing, almost synaesthetic experiences seem important links in the poet's connection of Warhol and the destruction of the World Trade Centre.

As if the Mail Runner had entertained some notion of seafaring adventure, even at the money end of the shipping industry, he begins with a possible admission of disappointment: 'There was no languor, no drowsy trade winds, / or stoned-out stupor of lapping waves'. His voyage, in this, and the other related poems in the section, is simply by elevator. The further denial, 'I was no Ishmael', summons Melville's *Moby-Dick*, as well as the Book of Genesis. The Biblical Ishmael was Abraham's first son by the young slave-woman, Hagar, and is an important prophet of Islam. Unlike the narrator of *Moby-Dick*, the poet is not a wanderer in 'the wilderness of the water' and has yet to discover his potential narrative.

Connected through his parents' family to the Armenian genocide, Peter Balakian is a writer intensely committed, in poetry and prose memoir, to the concept of witness. In this poem, he achieves a convincing tone of youthful detachment. The 'Twin Towers' have as yet to enter history, and the young mail-runner sees himself insulated from corporate piracy, 'at the edge of a skyline of money, / rising in a glass box'.

Light, air and 'gearless traction in transparency' are evoked in the syntax, sometimes, abbreviated, and the structuring in two- and three-line stanzas. It's as if we're shown the internal organs of the towers, the tracery of the grillage, rather than the undecorated blocky exteriors. The 'whiff of 4-martini lunches' evokes the scent of a now-proscribed free-market euphoria. Acute sensory response testifies to the excitement of the ascent, culminating in an epiphany 'at the 85th in a sky lobby' in a flood of transforming sunshine. Originally from New Jersey, Balakian presents the panoramic view of his home state in terms of indistinct brightness and distance, an expression, in the penultimate stanza, of purely aesthetic interest – 'just gouache and platinum coming apart – / a glistening smudge'.

In his storeyed box of light, the protagonist's seems pleased with the wealth of contrasts, confidently allowing them to float and cohere. The amused but important connection of the physical experience to Gaston Bachelard's *The Poetics of Space* contrasts interestingly with concluding quotation from Theodore Roethke's poem of deep personal crisis, 'The Lost Son'.

Perhaps readers need to recall Roethke's earlier lines ('A lively understandable spirit / Once entertained you') to sense the guarded emotional energy now 'circulating the air'.

Later, in the collection's central sequence, *A-Train / Ziggurat / Elegy,* Balakian summons Ovid: 'Omens… are wont to wait upon beginnings' (19). The events and images of 9/11 are inextricably present in 'World Trade Center / Mail

Runner / '73'. Even the phrase 'the heroism of stair-climbing' evokes, besides Bachelard, the firefighters and others who lost their lives on the choking stairways of the towers.

'The artist should be a whole working person', Balakian told his interviewer in *The Courtland Review*. The power of the poems in *Ziggurat* is in the range of experiences and knowledge they respond to, the linguistic energies deployed and the skill with which the narrative is layered, allowing personal memory and historical commentary to permeate the present moment.

https://www.theguardian.com/books/2015/mar/09/ peter-balakian-world-trade-center-mail-runner-73-poem-week

YVES BONNEFOY

The Light, Changed

translated by John Naughton

We no longer see each other in the same light,
We no longer have the same eyes, the same hands.
The tree is closer, and the water's voice more lively,
Our steps go deeper now, among the dead.

God, who are not, put your hand on our shoulder,
Rough cast our body with the weight of your return,
Finish blending our souls with these stars,
These woods, these bird cries, these shadows and these days.

Give yourself up in us the way fruit tears apart,
Have us disappear in you. Reveal to us
The mysterious meaning in what is merely simple
And would have fallen without fire in words without love.

La Lumière, Changée

Nous ne nous voyons plus dans la mème lumière
Nous n'avons plus les mèmes yeux, les memes mains,
L'arbre est plus proche, et la voix des sources plus vive,
Nos pas sont plus profonds, parmi les morts.

Dieu qui ne pas, pose ta main sur notre épaule,
Ébauche notre corps du poids de ton retour,
Achéve de meler à nos âmes ces astres,
Ces bois, ces cries d'oiseaux, ces ombres et ces jours.

Renonce-toi en nous comme un fruit se déchire,
Efface-nous en toi. Découvre-nous
Le sense mystérieux de ce qui ne'est que simple
Est fût tombé san feu dans des mots sans amour.

'The Light, Changed' ('La Lumière, Changée') is originally from Yves Bonnefoy's 1965 collection, *Pierre* Écrite (*Words in Stone*), a selection of which is reprinted in Carcanet's dual-text collected poems, *Yves Bonnefoy, 1:Poems* (edited by Anthony Rudolf, with John Naughton and Stephen Romer, and contributions from six others).

The collection opens with John Naughton's English translation of 'The Tombs of Ravenna', a prose meditation Bonnefoy composed in 1953. It reveals the younger poet's already intense preoccupation with the concept of unity between stone and light. The experience of visiting these tombs (Dante's tomb is one of them) was deeply imprinted on his memory: '… I go back in my mind towards Ravenna as to the source of a light… In Ravenna, nothing tarnishes the purity of the great burst of light, without which, as I have learned, one cannot live'.

In the series of highly-charged short poems of *Words in Stone,* it's as if the mystical and aesthetic qualities of the tombs were re-formed. Stone becomes 'a stone', humble and earthy. Love-poems, as many seem to be, are almost 'Revelations of Divine Love' (to borrow the words of Julian of Norwich), filtered through the sacrament of marriage, or physical relationship conceived as sacrament. Many have an addressee, and, in the first group of the series, 'The Lamp, The Sleeper', this figure appears as some kind of saviour. The form of the second-person plural pronoun used in the French text is the intimate one. The figure addressed, though a presence of great power and comfort, might exist as a presence only in the speaker's imagination, burning there like a lamp during a dark night. In a group of poems in which the title of each is simply 'Une Pierre', each stone becomes the speaker: it may also represent God, an animal, the earth itself. The identity is always fluid, death-haunted. One of the 'stone' poems, consisting of a single couplet, is especially beautiful in Naughton's translation: 'Fall but softly rain upon this face. / Put out the humble clay lamp slowly.' ('Tombe, mais douce pluie, sur le visage. / Éteins, mais lentement, le très pauvre chaleil.')

'The Light, Changed' is placed towards the end of the series, and its opening, gently punning assertion, 'We no longer see each other in the same light' could initially suggest that a mature, no-longer-idealised stage in a romantic relationship had been reached. The lovers have shared a commitment for many years, and feel impelled, now that their 'steps…go deeper…among the dead', to renew their sacrament. Since, for the spokesperson, God does not exist, there has to be a new kind of sacrament, revealed through matter. However, 'we' could represent a bigger collective, a congregation that encompasses a nation, or humanity itself at a stage of evolution perceived as late and endangered. Then, like a secular 'translation' of the traditional Lord's Prayer, the poem becomes a plea murmured on behalf of us all.

The second stanza invites the 'Dieu qui n'est pas' to return. Presence is evoked through weight and proximity – the density of 'these' stars and woods and the contrastingly weightless 'bird cries' and shadows. The speaker implores God to 'finish blending our souls' with these elements, significantly adding 'days' to his list. Translating the verb 'ébauche' into 'rough cast', Naughton inventively combines the idea of making a rough outline with an actual substance, the builder's roughcast. The poem suggests our organic resorption into nature is somehow un-satisfactory: as a process, it requires an end product, a point of complete existence and rest (stone, instead of stones).

Paradox is at the core of Bonnefoy's imaginative intelligence – that of the philosopher, mathematician and literary theorist as well as poet. Sam Sacks has written interestingly in *The New Yorker* about the poet's 'American side' and his culture-transcending solution to the question, 'Could poetry both freely create and rationally assert?' Perhaps, in answer, Bonnefoy continues to draw on his earlier Surrealist influences. In the third stanza of 'The Light, Changed', a startling simile almost intrusively re-shapes the non-God: 'Give yourself up in us the way fruit tears apart.' A reader can more easily go along with the idea of being blent into stars and woods by a God-shaped force of nature, than with the idea of God as a fruit which is torn, chewed, swallowed, digested. Transubstantiation has rarely been evoked with such delicious, juicy, invigorating coarseness. And it's a two-way metaphor, reversed when the speaker demands that 'we' too should be effaced, consumed.

Bonnefoy, as Sacks says, unites opposites: he succeeds in grounding the dream, and fluently moving between the symbolic and physical. 'God, who are not, put your hand on our shoulder' reveals the process in a nutshell. Physicality wins easily over abstraction in those fleshly, almost stone-solid images of 'your hand' and 'our shoulder'. At the end of the poem, we shift again into the more abstract realm, but the abstractions are made to glow through the word which best mediates between abstract and concrete: fire. 'Reveal to us / The mysterious meaning in what is merely simple / And would have fallen without fire in words without love.' ('Découvre-nous / le sens mystérieux de ce qui n'est que simple / Et fût tombé sans feu dans des mots sans amour.')

https://www.theguardian.com/books/booksblog/2018/feb/05/poem-of-the-week-the-light-changed-by-yves-bonnefoy

ANNE STEVENSON

The Miracle of the Bees and the Foxgloves

Because hairs on their speckled daybeds baffle the little bees,
Foxgloves hang their shingles out for rich bumbling hummers,
Who crawl into their tunnels-of-delight with drunken ease
(See Darwin's pages on his foxglove summers)
Plunging over heckles caked with sex-appealing stuff,
To sip from every hooker an intoxicating liquor
That stops it propagating in a corner with itself.

And this is how the foxglove keeps its sex life in order.
Two anthers – adolescent, in a hurry to dehisce –
Let fly too soon, so pollen lies in drifts about the floor.
Along swims bumbler bee and makes an undercoat of this,
Reverses, exits, lets it fall by accident next door.
So ripeness climbs the bells of *Digitalis* flower by flower,
Undistracted by a mind, or a design, or by desire.

October 15th was 'Ada Lovelace Day', founded in 2009 by Suw Charman-Anderson to celebrate women's achievements in science, technology, engineering and mathematics. Ada Lovelace (1815–52) was a gifted mathematician and pioneer theorist of artificial intelligence. As the daughter of Lord Byron, perhaps she should also represent the science-inspired poets now enriching our cultural ecosystem? A significant number of these are women, among them Anne Stevenson, who was mining that particular seam long before today's gold-rush. In 'The Miracle of the Bees and the Foxgloves' from her collection, *Astonishment*, it's the intricacies of foxglove pollination which delight both her analytical mind and her imagination.

'See Darwin's pages on his foxglove summers' the 4th line advises, an elegant footnote incorporated into the poem's text. The pages can be found in Charles Darwin's 1876 study, *The Effects of Cross- and Self-Fertilisation in the Vegetable Kingdom*. In his section on *Digitalis purpurea* (L), or Common Foxglove, Darwin stresses that it's only 'the larger humble-bees' which participate in the plant's fertilisation. So the sonnet begins with a reminder of that conclusion, translated into glowing metaphor: 'Because hairs on their speckled daybeds baffle the little bees, / Foxgloves hang out their shingles for rich bumbling hummers'. Darwin's 'humble-bee' and the more familiar term, 'bumblebee', verbally cross-fertilise to produce 'rich bumbling hummers', a description encapsulating the insect's sounds, movement and cushiony, gilded plumpness. The relationship of foxglove to bee is densely honeycombed with metaphors of seduction. The flowers are 'speckled daybeds' and 'tunnels-of-delight'. Plied with nectar, the client-bees visit 'every hooker' in an intoxicated ecstasy

The word 'hooker' has a function beyond the metaphorical. Inside the foxglove flower are hairs which, like small hooks, help the bee gain foothold as 'he' climbs. For the reader, internal rhymes imitate the effect. 'Hooker', for example, leads to a near-rhyme with 'liquor' at the end of line 6. In the previous line 'heckles' (a form of 'hackles') also denoting an uneven surface, similarly connects in an internal near-rhyme with 'speckled'. The 'k' sounds add thickness to the summery weight of 'um' sounds. But the last line of the septet introduces a pragmatic note amid sensory entrancement. The nectar-lure has evolutionary purpose – to keep the foxglove from 'propagating in a corner with itself'. Darwin's comparative studies showed that cross-fertilised plants were frequently healthier than the self-fertilised.

Stevenson restructures the harmonious machinery of the sonnet into two septets, adding a further refinement, a (mostly) seven-beat line. A little lighter on internal rhymes, though still finding delicate inner sound patterns, the second septet maintains and develops the sexual drama. The anthers 'let fly' their pollen prematurely, and 'Along swims bumbler bee and makes an undercoat of this'. The nicknaming informality here add piquancy to the poet's voice, and generates a shared creaturely warmth. Darwin's own language is anthropomorphic at times, with words like 'carry', 'crawl', 'footholds', 'ease'. The poem's linguistic abundance makes room for every-day domestic nouns like 'daybeds' and 'undercoat', faintly slangy idioms and the naturalist's precise vocabulary ('anthers', 'dehisc', '*Digitalis*') when necessary.

The task of the poet as science-writer is not simply to observe, describe and add figurative colouring, but to trace a narrative without over-dramatisation. Here, the consummation when 'ripeness climbs the bells of *Digitalis* flower by flower' is beautifully casual, and the almost throw-away last line gives the poem its intellectual power when it tells us the transformation has occurred 'Undistracted by a mind, or a design, or by desire'.

The reader may have relished a vision of both 'design' and 'desire' in the relations the poet has explored between bees and flowers. The title adverted to a 'miracle', after all. Now the scientist might seem to be throwing cold water on the poet's satisfying and beautiful elaborations. But this would be a misunderstanding. What the poem tells us is that a perfectly functioning system has evolved without mind or design, and this is the miracle. It's a reminder that Creationism doesn't only risk denying the science – it mislays some of the astonishment.

https://www.theguardian.com/books/booksblog/2013/oct/21/poem-of-the-week-anne-stevenson

MAURICE RUTHERFORD

The Autumn Outings

That autumn I was quick getting away:
        only about
one-twenty on the rain-drenched Wednesday
I locked the premises and motored out,
all staff sent home, all workshop plant closed down,
all sense of any kind of business gone,
and not until I'd driven fifteen miles
along fast-flooding roads back into town,
past rival complexes just clinging on,
did rain let up and vision clear: those files

I'd never see again; that desk, the phone
        that shrilled all day
when first it was installed; not hear the moan
compressors made, be soothed by lathes, nor say
'Good morning George, alright?', or 'Nice one, Bert',
the human touch, no more, not to distract
them too long from their work, but just enough
to let them see I cared, and not to hurt
old feelings as I tried to breast the fact
of cancelled orders, creditors turned rough.

The friendly bank soon bared its teeth – drew blood;
        and then that bane,
the Tax Man, claimed his pound. And so, the flood.
(fine detail dims again as, too, the pain
recedes three autumns on; yet loss stays true.)
The rain comes vicious now –wipers full speed,
dipped headlights on, rear fogs – the journey seems

to lengthen every time I live it through,
involuntarily, as when the need
for sleep is scuppered by recurring dreams.

My crowd was breast-fed clichés, meal on meal:
        to pull its weight,
nose to the grindstone, shoulder to the wheel,
and, once it stepped inside the factory gate,
was wedded to its work; slapped all the time
by Newbolt's hand: *Play up, and play the game.*
Well, this sounds fine; but what about the bloke
who's anorexic, short-nosed, cannot climb
to reach the wheel, and never makes the team?
For him such wedding tales are guffs of smoke.

Again the morning paper hits the floor –
        banner headlined
PIT CLOSURES SHOCK – and umpteen thousand more
are facing broken marriages to mines.
A few, lured by that bit-of-fresh, fool's gold,
pin hopes on boarding-houses, market-stalls;
one man sits out his protest down the pit,
while lefties call for strikes with all the old
clenched-fist salutes, and aerosol the walls:
SCARGILL FOR KING and TARZAN IS A SHIT.

Their first few days of idleness will see
        in those it hits
undreamed-of traits in personality:
some will get by and others go to bits;
the strong become the weak, the weak make good
as quickly as it's said. Then, as the days
stack up to months or, as in my case, years,

high principles get trampled in the mud
where guile and self-survival point new ways
to quick back-pocket jobs, fiddles and fears

of being caught. But fears will yield, in time,
        a sort of pride,
though not the social pride that saw men climb
from old-world swamps: a sense that one's defied
the odds, the system; finger-licked the crème,
nose-thumbed some top brass, bested those who made
the rules and all the running. What survives?
Of Us: too early yet to tell. Of Them:
'Indifferents and Incapables'; their trade
in UB40s and P45s.

In brass-lined boardrooms up and down the land
        deep in regret
a million more redundancies get planned,
while chairmen's hiked-up salaries are set,
and Urban Councils chase arrears in rents.
Wide-boys, insider-dealers, some M.P.s
grow richer by a second home in Spain,
a custom-plated white Mercedes Benz,
that new portfolio. True-blue disease.
The spores of loss, somewhere becoming gain.

Maurice Rutherford's work is attractively down-to-earth in tone, soft-spoken in a dry, faintly melancholy, Northern English way. His themes, whether historical or personal, are handled with warmth and common sense, and an easily overlooked formal fluency. A political edge is often present, though not usually as plainly declared as in his 1992 *tour de force*, 'The Autumn Outings'.

A native of Hull, and a near-contemporary of Philip Larkin, Rutherford sometimes uses Larkinesque forms or turns-of-phrase for his own poetic purposes. It's as if he simply found that Larkin liberated his own ideas. 'The Autumn Outings' is different, a class-critique which subverts Larkin as a lament for social catastrophe composed in the optimistic, ode-like stanza of 'The Whitsun Weddings'.

In Larkin's poem, you'll remember, a detached narrator describes almost novelistically the train-travelling wedding parties: he makes them comic, even bucolic, yet allows them to inhabit a landscape that, however mundane, is lit with a vague sense of possibility. The poem culminates in that famous, mysterious epiphany: 'And as the tightened brakes took hold, there swelled / A sense of falling, like an arrow-shower / Sent out of sight, somewhere becoming rain.'

The journey in 'The Autumn Outings' is a lonely, silent, often-repeated one. The narrator, whose own company has gone bust, begins by remembering how he drove away from the closed-down plant in pouring rain. The large stanza is utilised not only for a discursive narrative but for impassioned complaint. This is an angry poem, quietly but pointedly bitter about managerial greed and exploitation, and it remains a stringent comment on current values.

For all the references to 'The Whitsun Weddings', it has more serious aims than parody. The references are partly structural, and pathos rather than comedy emerges from the grammatical parallels. But the most important 'hinge' between the two poems is the notion of 'wedding', which Rutherford plays with to considerable effect. His poem certainly does not deny the wedding couples of Larkin's epithalamium their right to fun and happiness, but it exposes a different, darker dimension of working-class life. The harsh reality is that a man must be 'wedded' to his work – until, of course, his work decides to divorce him.

The speaker, unlike Larkin's narrator, is very much part of his community. He has been a good boss, as the second stanza reveals , and, even in extremis, he thinks compassionately of his employees. Time moves on with the poem, and stanza 5 unfurls a complaint against Michael Heseltine's infamous pit closures in the early 1990s. It turns out that the speaker has remained jobless for years. Now he muses on the general effects of unemployment, including the deterioration of his own high principles in favour of 'quick back-pocket jobs'. The 'fat cats' are the most culpable, but they are not the only fallible people in this poem.

'The Autumn Outings' rises to a trenchant climax. As at the beginning of the poem, the rhyme-sounds insist we hear a commentary on Larkin. The transcendental conclusion of his poem helps underline the stingingly political implications of Rutherford's, in which he imagines 'the spores of loss, somewhere becoming gain'.

Rutherford is a master craftsman. His work should be far better known, but it belongs to a seam of English poetry that recent critics have neglected to mine – post-Movement, perhaps, rather than post-modern, working-class but not wearing its class on its sleeve in the more showy 'them and uz' manner of Tony Harrison.

'The Autumn Outings' originally appeared in Rutherford's 1994 collection, *Love is a Four-Letter World*, published by the (sadly) no-longer-trading Peterloo Poets. It's included in *And Saturday is Christmas: New and Selected Poems*, Shoestring, 2010.

https://www.theguardian.com/books/booksblog/2009/dec/21/ poem-of-the-week-maurice-rutherford

VLADIMIR MAYAKOVSKY

Ay, But Can Ye?

translated by Edwin Morgan

Wi a jaup the darg-day map's owre-pentit –
I jibbled colour frae a tea-gless;
Ashets o jellyteen presentit
To me the gret sea's camshach cheek-bleds.
A tin fish, ilka scale a mou –
I've read the cries o a new warld through't.
But you
Wi denty thrapple
Can ye wheeple
Nocturnes frae a rone-pipe flute?

Scots-English Glossary
jaup – splash, slap
darg-day – work-day
owre-pentit – painted over
jibbled – dribbled, splashed
gless – glass
ashets – dishes
jellyteen – gelatine
camshach – crooked
cheek-bleds – cheek-bones
ilka – each
mou – mouth
denty – dainty
thrapple – windpipe
wheeple – whistle feebly
rone-pipe – spout for rainwater

вы могли бы?

Я сразу смазал карту будня,
плеснувши краску из стакана;
я показал на блюде студня
косые скулы океана.
На чешуе жестяной рыбы
прочел я зовы новых губ.
А вы
ноктюрн сыграть
могли бы
на флейте водосточных труб?

Edwin Morgan's translations of Vladimir Mayakovsky into Scots are justly admired, and who better that these two brilliantly innovative poets to mark the centenary of Russia's October Revolution? Like the revolutionary poets (in fact, as something of one himself) Edwin Morgan believed that literary movements 'should serve the ends of life as well as the ends of art' (Introduction, *Sovpoems*, 1961). Written in 1913, Mayakovsky's poem, 'вы могли бы?' asks one of the earliest questions which revolution will pose for writers: what sort of art can be distilled from, and equal to, the new order? At this stage it's more precisely an aesthetic than ethical question, and perhaps it includes a young poet's question-to-self.

Mayakovsky joined the Social Democratic Labour Party at the age of 15. His activism resulted in several prison sentences, and he began writing poetry during a spell of solitary confinement. Poetry and revolution had got inextricably tangled into one, he noted in his autobiography *I, Myself.* In 'Ay, But Can Ye?' the creative challenge is acutely, if humorously, perceived, and a lot of artistry goes into its brief formulation.

Morgan brings out sonorities audible in the Russian but beyond the scope of standard English. He even interpolates additional touches of assonance. For example, there's a single unrhymed line in the original, the one in which Mayakovsky challenges his audience (or himself) about the performing of nocturnes. He wants to strike a flat, unmusical note at this point. Morgan, contrastingly, brings in an extra, mischievous echo with his 'thrapple / wheeple' couplet.

The fruitful ambiguity of the Russian language thrusts the translator immediately aboard the Lingo-Waltzer. Various conjunctions would be acceptable in the title, each bringing a subtle shift of emphasis: 'And can you?', 'But can you?', 'So can you?' Morgan's solution is rather more combative, with that additional 'Ay' suggesting a laconic riposte to an over-confident claim: *yeah right, you think you can, but let's see.*

The poem's first-person, past-tense narrative springs a surprise. Mayakovsky, it seems, might have already made his poem and proven himself capable of the task. He has 'suddenly smeared the weekday map' in the English version, which is closer to the original first line than Morgan's, and conjures outlandish and arresting images from everyday things. The tea-glass (*stakan* in Russian means a tall glass) seems to contain liquid paint, and the splashing onto the plate of fish-jelly transforms it into an ocean with 'crooked cheek-bones'. This richly physical metaphor turns food into art, and synaesthetically mixes up tasty sounds with surreal images. The setting may be homely, but Mayakovsky's version of the domestic is a new playground where art trips, muddles and 'smears' the bourgeois order.

Morgan chooses a Scots word which means 'crooked' in preference to 'slanted' (both possible) to describe the sea's cheek-bones, and makes his own thick harmonies in 'the gret sea's camshach cheek-bleds'. His four-beat lines, a little jumpier than Mayakovsky's, cleverly re-invent the ABBA rhyme scheme, energising it with unexpected verbs ('owre-pentit', 'presentit').

In the next segment, the poets assert their fidelity to the new ideals. Morgan, on this occasion, creates a particularly weird and striking image, turning the fish-scales into 'mouths' ('ilka scale a mou –') as if going all out to 'make strange' as the Russian formalists advised. Mayakovsky seems more restrained in his reference to reading 'the cries of new lips' on the fish-scales.

While some commentators have linked the image of the fish with Cubist art, the more likely reference is a shop-sign. The fish combines comedy and horror in Morgan's emphases: it demands a particular response to a 'new warld' which cannot exclude all commerce. It's now that Morgan fleshes out the 'you' with extra description (and the additional rhyme-sounds), so as to emphasise the artistic challenge: 'But you / Wi denty thrapple / Can ye wheeple / Nocturnes fra a rone-pipe flute?' In summoning a listener cursed with a dainty windpipe, Morgan introduces a more explicitly anti-aristocratic critique. His use of Scots has lifted the poem out of the poetry-class (in both senses). Now he seems to glare scornfully at the timid and over-educated aesthetes. The question of the title takes on the full weight of its difficulty: can you honestly play nocturnes on a rain-pipe? And should you try? What other, truer music will you invent?

Morgan's Scots has different registers. It's literary as well as colloquial. Contrast the phonetically spelled 'Jellyteen' with the French-flavoured 'ashets' (from 'assiettes'). The linguistic paint-jibbling is an abundantly varied source of colour.

'Ay, But Can Ye?' appears in Morgan's *Collected Translations*, a modern classic which features a grand variety of poets. For more of Mayakovsky in Scots, Morgan's volume *Wi the Hail Voice* (Carcanet, 2016) is essential reading.

https://www.theguardian.com/books/2017/oct/16/poem-of-the-week-ay-but-can-ye-by-vladimir-mayakovsky

LEAH FRITZ

Going, Going…

At this tail-end that might unwind a longer tale
than I would care to tell, how vividly I see,
under the microscope's unfocused lens, the child
I was and, viewed through sharper eyes, I still may be,
wriggling on the slippery slide on which I'm caught,
none the wiser in this, than that, lost century.

Born with, though not quite silver, nonetheless a spoon
to overfeed my avid mouth – that I now find
myself your specimen is no catastrophe
perhaps, but I do feel a victim, and I mind
my length of life, assiduously extended
by right attitudes, has got me in this bind.

You find yourself impatient with my sentences
which start out one way, turn around and start again
most often in the middle; then, just when you think
there's no hope of an ending, suddenly do end –
but some place in the middle, yet again. A dash
will do, as in 'I must' – and dash I would, my friend,

if only… Slowly do I rise and slowly sit,
and those who face a working day each morning sigh
when offering their hard-won seats on buses to the
likes of me. Embarrassed, I'd rather stand, but try
as I might with smiles and all five feet of solid
inner pride, it's the outer me I can't deny.

As if I am an actor made to play the part,
and nature applied the putty and the grease-paint,
I walk out on the stage, an extra in the scene,
to no applause. Indeed, I feel I am a faint
shadow in the backdrop, something that the artist
tried unsuccessfully to hide, something too quaint

for the production that the playwright had in mind.
And so is this alexandrine, a rhythm slow
yet jogging quite irregularly, like the walk
of one unsure of how or where she's meant to go.
Wherever, however, it's not the way I'd choose.
Odds on, I bet my life that I will get there, though.

'Going, going' by the American-born, octogenarian poet, Leah Fritz, was the title poem of her 2007 collection, and is included in her latest, *Whatever Sends the Music into Time: New and Selected Poems*.

Growing older, in the narrator's words, is 'no catastrophe', but it's an unsettling experience that can shake the most solidly founded identity. Fritz charts the physical effects and, particularly, the psychological shifts entailed, with wry humour and a firm technical grip. The metre is the alexandrine, traditionally the standard, 12-syllable unit of French prosody. It has a slow, slightly choppy rhythmic effect in English, 'like the walk / of one unsure of how or where she's meant to go'. The stanzas are all sextains, with lines 2, 4 and 6 sharing a full rhyme, and 1, 3 and 5 unrhymed. Although the line is syllabic, the rhymes create a contrastingly accentual effect. Contrast is the core of this poem.

The first-person narrator is keenly aware of the tension between how she is seen and how she sees herself. Sometimes she borrows the 'sharper eyes' of a perhaps judgemental, and rather less perceptive, other. She may be amused by the bafflement she causes, or resentful at being patronised. The 'I' has a strong voice and presence: the 'you' is more of a mystery.

A medical investigation might be suggested in the opening stanzas: there are the microscope and slide, and the loss of status implied by 'your specimen' and 'a victim'. 'You' could be a doctor, perhaps. But a more ambitious and metaphorical reading would be that the speaker is addressing society in general: 'You' could include the readers of the poem, or embody the speaker's other, younger selves. Either way, she feels reduced by her auditor to 'the child I was', a shrinkage taken to surreal and witty extremes in imagery that goes back to the cellular beginnings of life, to a minute, trapped being 'wriggling' like a spermatozoon under a microscope.

In the next stanza, the remembered child relishes the spoon that 'overfeeds my avid mouth'. A political critique of Western values is intimated. The irony (and punishment?) is that privileged birth and 'right attitudes' lead to long life and so to that inescapable 'bind' of extended age.

De-familiarisation is expressed in puns, such as the 'tail-end' and 'longer tale' of the first line, and the double interpretations possible of 'slippery slide' and 'mind'. In the third stanza, the speaker seems rather to enjoy her hearer's impatience with the way she constructs her sentences, and she demonstrates the poetic skill of pausing 'in the middle' by placing, twice, the word 'middle' mid-line. It's implied that subtleties like the punctuation of 'a dash', depend on transcription: the reader sees two dashes, in fact. Again, the poet takes advantage of the pun: 'and dash I would, my friend, // if only'. It carries her into a new setting – a crowded morning bus-ride.

In a curiously poignant exchange, one person reluctantly gives up his seat, and the other reluctantly gives up her pride. The smiling social mask hides anger, perhaps, and certainly a profoundly doubled identity. The dismissive idiom, 'the likes of me', is self-mockingly appropriated, and a line-break after the definite article, so the accent falls on 'likes', emphasises the dislocation ('The / likes of me').

In the fifth stanza, the part the speaker has to play is not the one Shakespeare so shockingly describes, 'sans everything'. Fritz's player is from a culture and period where at least some of the losses of old age can be remedied, but where such players generally cease to be visible, and recede to 'a faint / shadow in the backdrop'. The narrator has travelled from the awareness of being a closely observed 'specimen' to 'something that the artist / tried unsuccessfully to hide'.

But she, too, is an artist. Although the alexandrine metre is claimed to be 'too quaint', it represents a conscious artistic decision. Both the poet and the metre know where they're going. In fact, the poem has consistently reconstructed the self, contrasting the uncertainties of living in time and human skin with the sturdiness of form and syntax.

There has been no indulgence in blame, bitterness or self-pity. The speaker has delivered no lectures. She has simply offered an insider's un-illusioned view of age, and made it clear that the going is tough – interestingly and even amusingly tough, but tough all the same. She readily concedes that 'it's not the way I'd choose'. And then she delivers a bracing, almost throw-away punch-line: 'Odds on, I bet my life that I will get there, though.' It's a wry joke, with a hard truth embedded in the idiomatic word-play, a punch-line more than worthy of the name.

*https://www.theguardian.com/books/2011/aug/22/
poem-of-the-week-leah-fritz*

EILÉAN NÍ CHUILLEANÁIN

The Words Collide

The scribe objects. You can't put it like that,
I can't write that. But the client
is a tough small woman forty years old.
She insists. She needs her letter
to open out full of pleated revolving silk
and the soft lobes of her ears
where she flaunts those thin silver wires.

She wants to tell her dream to the only one
who will get the drift. How she saw their children lying
every one dressed out in their simplest fears. They glowed,
the shape of their sentence outlined in sea green.
Among those beloved exiles
one sighed happy, as a curtain
lightened and the grammar changed, and the wall
showed pure white in the shape of a bird's wing.

But when she whispered it to the scribe he frowned
and she saw she had got it wrong, she had come
to a place where they all spoke the one language:
it rose up before her like a quay wall
draped in sable weeds. He said,
you can't put those words into your letter.
It will weigh too heavy, it will cost too much,
it will break the strap of the postman's bag,
it will crack his collarbone. The bridges
are all so bad now, with that weight to shift
he's bound to stumble. He'll never make it alive.

This poem, from the closing pages of Eiléan Ní Chuilleanáin's latest collection, *The Boys of Bluehill*, forms a web of intriguing metaphors. The question of what is literal and what isn't is part of its beguilement. It begins with an apparently realistic scene between the scribe and his female client. The designation 'Scribe' suggests other times or cultures, but the man is immediately recognisable as the official type, hard of heart and blunt of speech: 'You can't put it like that.' That tells us enough. The woman is given more of a presence, and it seems as if her singling out might indicate that she looks a little different from other women around her. She's visibly 'tough' but there's no conflict between that quality (which many women in urban cultures tend to conceal) and the residual femininity of the silver wires in her ears. She has a wholeness of being that, along with her inability to read and write, suggests a rural background.

The first stanza presents an antagonism which might be metonymic – native culture against migrant, state versus individual, rule-keepers against innovators. With the description of what the woman wants – or, as the poem rather more significantly says, *needs* – the diction flowers into metaphor. The image of a letter that will 'open out full of pleated folds of silk / and the soft lobes of her ears' is beautiful and almost unguardedly sexual. Its origami suggests words as both art and body-parts, words whose art can recreate the 'pleated folds of silk' and 'soft lobes' of the erotic body. This intended letter must be a love-letter, so personal and so richly designed as to present the physical woman to her husband or lover: it will almost be a surrogate sex-act, joining the separated couple.

We learn in the next stanza how close the woman is to the recipient. She wants both to confide her sexual need for him and to impart a dream she has had. As the father of her children, he is 'the only one who will get the drift'. Placing the couple is complicated, but it seems that the woman has left home some time before. She and her husband share the same language, although she is unable to write it down. The children ('beloved exiles') may be with her, but they may be dispersed their separate ways.

From the idea of a letter that enacts her sexual dreaminess, we move swiftly to the nightmare image of an actual dream and 'How she saw their children lying / every one dressed in their simplest fears'. The children, it seems, have died during a long sea-voyage (a pun on 'drift' may have been indicated) – the voyage which has taken them into exile. 'They glowed, / the shape of their sentence outlined in sea green' seems at first too gentle and colourful description to be suggestive of death by drowning – until we remember this is a dream, with its own strange transformations.

Again, the imagery is sensuous and beautiful. It suggests the woman's artistry with words, and raises the question as to how much we're still in the metaphorical realm of language. The word 'sentence' adds ambiguity. But the stanza concludes without further reference to death or imprisonment. There's a solid vision of contentment ('one sighed happy') and the wall, which will appear in a menacing guise later on, is, for this particular child, white and wing-like, a symbol of a liberation whose source may, again, be part linguistic ('…the grammar changed'). Language in 'The Words Collide' seems to represent the two poles of an exile's experience, assimilation and alienation, as it also represents the expressive poles, correctness and brevity versus elaboration and luxuriance – which may, in turn, be associated with gender and the theory of l'ecriture feminine.

In the final stanza we're shown that the woman, in whispering her words, has made herself vulnerable; she has offered trust and deference to the scribe, but her whispers are met with a frown, followed by an extended string of objections. That the words she needs to say are too heavy and costly for transportation is represented with powerful literalism. The scribe, in a cumulative list, insists they will break the strap on the post-bag, then that they will 'crack' the post-man's collarbone (the poet makes sure we hear that 'crack' in the internal para-rhyme with 'break') and then, it seems, they will kill him. The scribe becomes momentarily human, perhaps, when he almost attempts an apology. The land is in some kind of trauma of dereliction: 'the bridges are so bad now'. The failure of the bridges contrasts with the power of that monolithic language, which 'rose up before her like a quay wall'. Is it because words as bridges have fallen into disrepair that the letter the woman needs to write will not be written? Metaphorical and even surreal in some of its devices, the poem's own freight seems ultimately political. The words collide in what seems essentially an unequal power struggle, and the harsh words of the scribe resonate beyond the soft flowerings of metaphor. 'He'll never make it alive' seems no longer to come from a stock of excuses. It's as if the scribe had found an actual and terrible truth.

https://www.theguardian.com/books/booksblog/2015/sep/28/ poem-of-the-week-the-words-collide-eilean-ni-chuilleanain

JEE LEONG KOH

In His Other House

In this house there is no need to wait for the verdict of history
And each page lies open to the version of every other.
— *Eiléan Ní Chuilleanáin, 'In Her Other House'*

In my other house too, books fill the floor-to-ceiling shelves,
not only books on stock markets, seven habits, ghost stories,
but also poetry, Arthur Yap, Cyril Wong, Alfian Sa'at,
and one who moved away and who wrote *Days of No Name.*

My father comes home from the power station. When rested
(and this is how I know this is not real) he reads to us again,
for the seventh time, Philip Jeyaretnam's *Abraham's Promise*
in a quiet voice, unbroken by a frightened young supervisor.

When he closes the book, my dead grandfather stirs heavily
and says a word or two, that really says he has been listening.
And my beloved, knowing his cue, jumps up from the couch
to clear the dishes, for, he says, dishes don't wash themselves.

Softly brightened by a feeling I do not hurry to identify,
I move to the back of him and put my arms around his waist.
His muscles twitch like the needle on a motorboat's dashboard
as he turns a bone china plate against a rough cotton cloth.

The light from the window looks like a huge, blank sea.
In this other house there will be time to fill it but right now
the bell intones in silver, and here, on a surprise night visit,
are my sister and her two daughters coming through the door.

Over Jee Leong Koh's new collection, *Steep Tea,* a pantheon of women poets hovers like a host of – no, not muses but – surrogate mothers. The epigraphs from these poets' works are often brief, no more than a couple of lines, but serve to underline a major theme or direction. Disposability is part of the attraction of his poetic mothers, Koh claims, but some of the writing has clearly served as midwife to his own imagination. In this week's poem, eloquent lines by the Irish poet, Eiléan Ní Chuilleanáin, help Koh to realise a perfect amalgamation of his two homes, the Singapore he left some twelve years ago and his adopted New York City.

In his blog, Song of a Reformed Headhunter (essential and delightful reading, which will tell you a good deal more about the poet and his many mothers), Koh writes that Eiléan Ní Chuilleanáin's poetry is 'populated by religious and folkloric motifs and so it reads like a world outside, beyond, beside, the ordinary world'. Koh's poem responds in an almost colloquial and certainly informal manner to her elevated yearning: '*In this house there is no need to wait for the verdict of history / And each page lies open to the version of every other.*' The 'page' metaphor is taken on and given 'a local habitation' in Koh's answering, but perhaps unexpected, first line. It should perhaps be read with a gentle, assenting emphasis on the possessive pronoun: 'In *my* other house too, books fill the floor-to-ceiling shelves' (my italics). That way, it reads not simply as a poet's monologue, but as a continuation of a poets' conversation.

Singaporean male writers figure large in this domestic Utopia. Koh builds the metaphor and compounds the political implications with a list of young favourites and senior mentors: the poet and painter Arthur Yap (1943–2006), Cyril Wong, Alfian Sa'at and Boey Kim Cheng, the author of *Days of No Name.* They are writers loved and valued by the poem's speaker for their radical vision, but whose work would, presumably, be little known or liked by his parents and grandparents – whose only books, pragmatic or populist, concern 'stock markets, seven habits, ghost stories'. In the fantasy 'other house' the writers loved by the son are part of the family's library. What's more, the father reads aloud to him, repeatedly, from an important work exploring post-independence difficulties with paternal identity – Philip Jeyaretnam's *Abraham's Promise*.

Koh's alternative inter-generational narrative allows the father a different history: he's able to rest after the day's work, and to read 'in a quiet voice, unbroken by a frightened young supervisor'. We're not told if the father was himself a victim of someone's unjust supervision, or whether he inflicted the destruction on himself in conformity to social or political demands. We know merely that, in the poem, he has recovered a lost, unbroken self. And Koh adds a further miracle – the dead grandfather, as if in a dream, is newly alive, listening, perhaps consenting.

This triad of reconciliation is occupied by a fourth male figure, the speaker's lover, who, a quiet onlooker, now starts on the washing up, with the affectionate, half-admonitory catchphrase of any mother or domesticated father in a conventional family, 'dishes don't wash themselves'. It somehow sets the seal on the group's contentment, like an acknowledgement that even an alternative dream-house can't run on literature alone. The sensation registered by the speaker as 'softly brightening' is one that beautifully illuminates these two concluding quatrains. Now we're shown significant small details, the twitch of the partner's muscles (the simile 'like the needle on a motorboat's dashboard' signals adventure and freedom beyond the washing up) and the wonderful contrast of movement and texture 'as he turns a bone china plate against a rough cotton cloth'. This graceful gesture is like the herald of a further level of reconciliation, bringing the sound of the door-bell 'in silver' and the arrival of three new night visitors, all female, into the fold.

Steep Tea celebrates family and friendship across their contemporary disconnections. The poet's physical mother is a distant but far from insignificant presence; she's a source of both depth and lightness, poignantly evoked in another favourite poem of mine, 'Singapore Buses are Very Reliable'. This poem's epigraph concerns Vladimir Nabokov: *'And they told him in Prague his mother died'* (Polina Barskova, 'Motherhood and Childhood').

Koh's poems reveal the enormous severances of exile. But loss and separation are only elements of the personal story he recounts: emigration enabled him to find himself both as a gay man and a poet. 'In His Other House' dreams up a place none of us, after all, emigrant or native, can bring into being (without learning how to stop time), a fusion of past and present, the reconciliation of old and new families. But a house where the light from the window suggests an ocean, one whose emptiness is undaunting and evokes a joyful confidence that 'there will be time to fill it' is never beyond the bounds of possibility. May every emigrant find it.

https://www.theguardian.com/books/booksblog/2015/sep/07/ poem-of-the-week-in-his-other-house-by-jee-leong-koh

DICK DAVIS

Political Asylum

My closest friends were killed. I have a life
That's comfortable in almost every way.
I haven't got a job yet, but my wife
Has found a good position with good pay –

Enough to keep us going anyway.
I don't go out much but, you see, my wife
Is out for almost all of every day.
I read a lot and reassess my life.

I've tried to write but what is there to say?
My friends were killed and this is now my life;
It's almost certain this is where we'll stay.
We like it here, especially my wife.

As both poet and translator, Dick Davis has produced work of a consistently high quality over a long career. His recently published volume, *Love in Another Language: Collected Poems and Selected Translations*, contains work from 1975 to the present, and demonstrates his ability to combine traditional form with naturalistic contemporary diction – not yet a lost art, but an increasingly rare one. The poems may be satirical, lyrical, wittily epigrammatic or elegiac: these are not necessarily separate categories, of course, because essential to Davis's art is a flexibility of tone. His speakers face some deep dark nights of the individual and family 'soul', but, however despondent, the craftsman-poet keeps chaos at bay. The tonal equilibrium is also an aspect of his strength as a translator: his translated poets come alive because that civil, quietly adaptable voice can contain their strange eloquence and help us hear it. Hafez, for example, speaks through Davis from a time and culture which seem not enormously far from our own, the voice clear and distinctive, the attitudes almost modern and never anachronistic.

Davis's profound and life-long intimacy with Persian poetry flows into his original poetry, too and provide subjects and nuances. It's impressive to get such a sense of organic wholeness from a poet's output, especially when it's as wide-ranging as this.

'Political Asylum' was first published in *Belonging* (2002). It might have an Iranian context (I chose it partly to connect readers with one of Davis's major subjects) but there is no reason in the poem to assume a particular setting or character. The speaker confides in us a little of his past, but his experience is not, after all, unusual or particular. There is room for readers to assign their chosen back-story.

He begins in a matter-of-fact tone, 'My closest friends were killed', and the rest of the narrative is similarly delivered in an unemotional manner. We learn he is a writer of a kind, a reader, and, at a hint from the second stanza, probably an intellectual. Now that he has been detached from his discipline and language by the war or revolution which killed his closest friends, his own life and actions have become his subject of study. His dilemma is presented in the first line, after the caesura. He doesn't say he is alive, but 'I have a life' so we immediately suspect how shallowly rooted, how unlike a real life, in fact, his existence is, although 'comfortable in almost every way'.

The smallness of the life is enacted in the technical constraints applied by the poem. In particular the cyclical recurrence of the rhymes 'life' and 'wife' suggests the hollowness of the redemption, and its distance from any real vitality. (He is sardonically aware of this, I think: the line-breaksoften seem to create small self-mocking qualifications of previous statements). There is another effect. The reiteration of the 'life /wife' rhymes, the repeated '-ay' rhymes, too, and the overall simple informality of the diction contribute to the impression that the narrator is not speaking his mother tongue. His colloquial English is perfect, but it's a lesser language than the one he requires. He doesn't own enough of it for it to express his real complexity. Occasionally, though, one has a sense of a physical gesture, perhaps a hand-signal, accompanying a particular word or phrase: 'anyway', 'you see', 'especially my wife'.

This wife is an important if ambiguous figure. As is repeatedly made clear, she has adapted well to the new circumstances – or, at least, that is how the speaker sees it. Her story may be as complicated as his, if in another way: perhaps a gulf has opened in the marriage, and her absences each day are not only related to work. What seems clear is that the poem's speaker feels a want of authority and choice. He is in psychological trouble. The reluctance to treat his experiences as a subject for writing, and the very thinness of his language in the poem, suggest that he will accomplish little in the project to reassess his life.

'Political Asylum' tells us that the losses of exile are not inevitably compensated by the attainment of physical safety and financial stability in an unreal 'new life'. The speaker's refuge is somehow too well-fenced. He has become trapped in it.

https://www.theguardian.com/books/booksblog/2018/mar/05/poem-of-the-week-political-asylum-by-dick-davis

MARIA TERESA HORTA

Poem

translated by Lesley Saunders

I let him come.
He sneaks on tiptoe
right up to my ear;

under its ribs my heart
quivers, quickens
as the excitement mounts:

first the forest appears,
then the woodland-sequel,
more mist than snow to the touch –

from the new poem's
very first line the paper sucks up
every waif-word

and an ugliness steals in,
a cunning hungry thing
crouching there incognito,

pretending to be tame and yet so wolfish
that he's the kernel of light
and then the noise of its cracking;

he's lithe on the path,
doubling back on himself,
running with the pack, loping alone;

pussy-footing through the night
he trails moonlight behind him
like a mink coat.

I feel him when the hairs on my skin
lift, and in the delicious dizziness
of my private pulse –

in the midst of my writing, in my dream-life,
I slip all his clothes slowly off
and slide him down beside me.

Poema

Deixo que venha
se aproxime ao de leve
pé ante pé até ao meu ouvido

Enquanto no peito o coração
estremece
e se apressa no sangue enfebrecido

Primeiro a floresta e em seguida
o bosque
mais bruma do que neve no tecido

Do poema que cresce e o papel absorve
verso a verso primeiro
em cada desabrigo

Toca então a torpeza e agacha-se
sagaz
um lobo faminto e recolhido

Ele trepa de manso e logo tão voraz
que da luz é a noz
e depois o ruído

Toma ágil o caminho
e em seguida o atalho
corre em alcateia ou fugindo sozinho

Na calada da noite desloca-se e traz
consigo o luar
com vestido de arminho

Sinto-o quando chega no arrepio
da pele, na vertigem selada
do pulso recolhido

À medida que escrevo
e o entorno no sonho
o dispo sem pressa e o deito comigo

Readers of a certain age will remember Maria Teresa Horta from an admired, and sometimes maligned, radical-feminist text of the early 1970s, *New Portuguese Letters (Novas Cartas Portuguesas).* With Maria Velho da Costa and Maria Isabel Barreno, Maria Teresa Horta formed the trio of writer-friends who came to be dubbed 'The Three Marias'. Their collaborative volume, known in English as *The Three Marias: New Portuguese Letters*, (tr. Helen R. Lane), was a multi-genre response to a seventeenth-century collection of letters allegedly written by a young nun, Mariana Alcoforado, to her absconding 'chevalier' lover. Horta had already received adverse criticism for her poetry, and the 'New Letters' were no sooner published than banned by the Portuguese government. A prosecution ensued, and the women faced jail sentences until, with the 1974 'carnation revolution', all charges were dropped.

Mariana Alcoforado had recovered her psychological independence through writing. The twentieth-century authors, with their collage of poems, fiction, letters and erotica, each work dated but unsigned, set out to assert their own female authenticity through solidarity. Lesley Saunders traces the source of her interest in Portuguese poetry to her first acquaintance with the 'New Letters', noting that it renewed her sense of 'what literature could accomplish, formally, as well as psychologically and politically'. Saunders was delighted finally to meet Maria Teresa Horta in Lisbon in 2015.

Her translation of Horta's new poem, 'Poema', won first prize in the Open category of the 2016 Stephen Spender Prize for Poetry in Translation. It combines sharp narrative clarity and an erotically charged, fairy-tale atmosphere. Saunders writes that she tried to reproduce the 'abbreviated, even dislocated, diction that disguises itself as something direct and uncomplicated'. By introducing punctuation into the English version, she underlines Horta's control of phrasing and tempo, and adds to the musical interest of our melody-resistant language.

The lineation has an excited tension in the first two stanzas. The wolf's presence is registered at once, but he quickly becomes elusive. It's in the third stanza that the mystery fully registers: 'first the forest appears, / then the woodland-sequel, / more mist than snow to the touch –'. The word 'sequel' contributes to the idea of the poem as story-telling, while the soft, crisp, tactile evocation of mist-damp forest and woodland suggests body-hair in different thicknesses and distribution. With the next stanza we go deeper into metaphor-land. The new poem has arrived, stealthy and 'incognito', and instantly 'the paper /

sucks up every waif-word'. It's an unfamiliar, maternal kind of animation: few poets see the language of their emergent poem as a vulnerable orphan.

Saunders finds similarities between Horta's 'Poema' and Ted Hughes's 'The Thought Fox': the difference is that 'Hughes' fox turns out to be the poet's poem; Horta's wolf emerges as the poem's poet'. Whoever 'he' is, I like the shifts in his character, and the general craftiness of his approach, 'pretending to be tame, and yet so wolfish'. It's recognised that the intimately known body – of man, woman or poem – may fall short of the ideal and even reveal a sudden 'ugliness' –a quality which, in the original poem, is a moral ugliness, depravity (*torpeza*). To receive the muse the artist may have to overcome revulsion. But perhaps what is most special about this wolf-muse is that he resists banal transformation. Saunders uses a wonderful, almost punning, feline metaphor, 'pussy-footing', in the eighth stanza, and darkens the trailed cape of moonlight, which is compared to 'ermine' in the original, 'mink' in the translation. This being is sometimes magical but he is always animal.

The narrative rises to a sensuous and role-reversing climax when the speaker undresses the newly passive creature: 'I slip all his clothes slowly off / and slide him down beside me.' At first seductive, finally seduced, the poem-wolf lies down with the poet-lamb. Saunders's translation reveals Horta's mature voice to have an easy, unapologetic authority. 'Poema' seems an important culmination and re-assertion of her status as an artist and radical thinker.

https://www.theguardian.com/books/booksblog/2016/nov/28/ poem-of-the-week-poema-by-maria-teresa-horta-translated-by-lesley-saunders

STANLEY MOSS

Visiting Star

I woke at sunrise,
fed my dogs, Honey and Margie –
to the east a wall of books and windows,
a lawn, the trees in my family,
the donkeys and forest behind the hill.
Sunlight showed itself in,
passed the China butterflies on the window
so birds watch out, don't break their necks.
On the back of a green leather chair for guests
facing me in sunlight and shadow, a sunlit Star of David,
two large handspans square.
I call my wife to see the star
she first thinks I painted on the chair.
Soon she catches on – no falling star.
We searched the room and outside.
How did the star come to be?
Without explanation. None.
The star visited a few minutes, disappeared,
or became invisible. Why?
I wondered if it was *le bel ajourd'hui*
or a holiday some Jews celebrate.
Playing fair, I told myself: watch out for
a crucifix anywhere before which
contrition saves condemned souls –
watch in the forest for portraits of the Virgin,
the wheel of Dharma down the road,
that teaches 'save all living beings,'
when the moon is full a crescent moon
reflected on a wall or lake.
Watch for flying horses!
I read the news of commandments broken.

Thou shalt not kill.
I write between the lines
Thou shalt not steal
seventy-five years from the life of a child.
Next day, I found my Star of David
was a glass sun and star reflection of
a tinkling shimmering wind chime made in China.
A pleasing, godless today fills my study.

'I'm a psalmist with a Miss-directed penis', declares the narrator in another poem in Stanley Moss's collection, *It's About Time*. Moss is sometimes termed a religious poet: if he is, he's one of the too-few irreligious kind, firmly of this world in his vivid pleasures and sorrows, joyfully harrying God from myth to unsatisfactory myth, denomination to denomination, fascinated by the whole subject of deity, but hardly expecting a catch or kill. He views the gods of the monotheist religions, as this poem will make clear, with a cynicism that's directed also towards their exegetes. While he quotes Auden with approval that 'all poets, as such / are polytheists', even this degree of mysticism is liable to subversion.

The narrative manner in 'Visiting Star' is typical of the rangy, idiomatic 'thinking aloud' style which imbues so much of Moss's work with its particular charm, even in the midst of lamentation. In some respects an oral poem, 'Visiting Star' is casual about commas, in fact the grammar in general is non-literary, speech-led. Moss is the easy-listening psalmist rather than the operatic kind.

This poem is 'on location', and nicely amplifies the collection's dedication *to departed friends, human, canine, arboreal, avian*. The author-speaker appears relaxed at the hub of an extended, inter-species network: his dogs have homely names, the trees, no less, are 'the trees in my family'. Civilised domesticity, with its books and picture-windows, is framed by the wider prospect of decreasingly tamed 'nature'. He has adjusted things to accommodate the untameable: this we learn from the reference to 'the China butterflies on the window / so birds watch out, don't break their necks'. It's a carefully-engineered, almost prelapsarian setting, where the sunlight is like a long-familiar neighbour who has 'showed itself in'. The trompe l'oeil, the visiting Star of David, significantly manifests itself on 'the back of a green leather chair for guests'.

At its first narrative climax, the poem shifts from leisurely past tense to the active engagement of the present: 'I call my wife.' Her reaction tells us that the Star of David is so clearly depicted she thinks it must be painted (happy thought that this is a household where husbands may paint pictures on expensive chairs and wives approve). But 'Soon she catches on – no falling star'. The poem reverts to the past historic, but continues to express the surprise and sense of a logical impasse; its urgent questions seem to have no answers. Religion, of course, is in the business of supplying answers: perhaps the poem is reminding us that 'negative capability' beats dogmatic interpretation any day. It's not a major loss, though still intriguing, when the star is discovered shortly to have mysteriously 'disappeared, / or become invisible'.

So far, there's no logical explanation, but the speaker is happy to think up illogical, mock-mystical ones. The tone is more playful than reverent when, after considering that the Star might have appeared because of some Jewish holiday, the observer reminds himself to watch out for manifestations from other religions like Christianity (the crucifix and the virgin Mary) and Islam (the crescent moon). He jokes that he's 'playing fair' and, yes, in reminding us of the human aura round the miraculous symbols, he is fairly apportioning blame and perhaps expressing disappointment. 'Watch out for flying horses', he wryly concludes.

Before solving the mystery, the narrative expands to consider religion's least soluble problem: the evil existent in a universe ordained by an omnipotent, all-loving God. For the beautiful, visiting stars of imaginative harmony co-exist with, might sometimes condone, the destruction of life: in Judaeo-Christian terms, the breaking of the sixth commandment. Moss re-phrases it, and renews its force, in terms of appalling theft which may be literal or psychological murder: '*Thou shalt not steal / seventy-five years from the life of a child.*' If the Star's symbolism is to be taken seriously, how does the epiphany square with the reality of bloodshed? This is an unexpected and powerful turn in the poem, carefully positioned before the denouement when, in the last four lines, the Star's origins are explained as the reflection cast by 'a tinkling, shimmering wind-chime made in China'. The poem rediscovers its earlier amused poise and delight, while the fiercely double-edged, Mallarmean concept of the 'beautiful today', alluded to in line 20, is gently echoed in the phrase 'pleasing, godless today'. Some of the pleasing-ness no doubt derives from the godlessness, though Moss is careful not to describe the day as 'pleasingly godless'. So atheism, as 'Made in China', enters and somehow guarantees the poem's attempt at a sacred synthesis (China, we may remember, was mentioned earlier in describing the bird-protecting butterflies). If it demolishes the miraculous, the joke of a 'communist' Star of David replenishes the idea of theologically open, ideology-free beatitude.

'Visiting Star' demonstrates that, without sentimentality or banality, old sacred stories can still be re-told, or their symbolism re-framed, with vitality, worldly realism and wit. Moss himself may be in the poem – a magus whose east comprises birds, trees, and animals seen through clear glass, and, of course, books. If God exists, the poem seems to suggest, 'he', too, might be both of, and in, the world more vividly than believers or atheists imagine. Moss rewrites the received ideas of religion and the religious poet: his psalms may be exactly the new songs needed to illuminate sombre new times

https://www.theguardian.com/books/booksblog/2015/dec/21/ poem-of-the-week-visiting-star-by-stanley-moss

FRANK ORMSBY

Fireflies

The lights come on and stay on under the trees.
Visibly a whole neighbourhood inhabits the dusk,
so punctual and in place it seems to deny
dark its dominion. Nothing will go astray,
the porch lamps promise. Sudden, as though a match
failed to ignite at the foot of the garden, the first squibs
trouble the eye. Impossible not to share
that sportive, abortive, clumsy, where-are-we-now
dalliance with night, such soothing restlessness.
What should we make of fireflies, their quick flare
of promise and disappointment, their throwaway style?
Our heads turn this way and that. We are loath to miss
such jauntiness in nature. Those fugitive selves,
winged and at random! Our flickery might-have-beens
come up from the woods to haunt us! Our yet-to-be
as tentative frolic! What do the fireflies say?
That loneliness made light of becomes at last
convivial singleness? That any antic spark
cruising the void might titillate creation?
And whether they spend themselves, or go to ground,
or drift with their lights out, they have left the gloom,
for as long as our eyes take to absorb such absence,
less than it seemed, as childless and deprived
as Chaos and Old Night. But ruffled too,
as though it unearthed some memory of light
from its long blackout, a hospitable core
fit home for fireflies, brushed by fireflies' wings.

Frank Ormsby's 'Fireflies' is a poem to brighten our darkness as 'the year's midnight' of the winter solstice approaches (December 22nd in the modern calendar). It's the title piece from the poet's 2009 collection, a volume whose main physical locations are the 'area of New York state' to which Ormsby has been a regular visitor over the years, and the Northern Ireland of his Enniskillen childhood and Belfast-based adult-life. But poems, of course, are not in thrall to borders, and this opening 'American' poem seems to extend the energies of the fireflies' 'antic spark' in many outer and inner directions.

The fireflies observed in the poem are themselves 'a whole neighbourhood'. They have their own rules and rituals, and there's a reliability to their apparent disorder, their nightly appearance 'so punctual and in place it seems to deny / the dark its dominion'. The narrative rhythm is smooth and steady-paced but elastic, stretching beyond the iambic pentameter it occasionally gestures towards, and settles for in the concluding lines. But the rhythm of the long middle segment of the poem is more staccato: it captures the fireflies' movement with short sentences, variously-placed caesurae, and emphatic punctuation. The exclamation marks spark like typographical fireflies.

Coined compounds such as 'where-are-we-now' and 'yet-to-be' form nice variations on the more familiar 'might-have-beens'. Used adjectivally, 'where-are-we-now' is the culminating surprise of an already surprising 8th line. In that dance of adjectives, the merry 'sportive, abortive' rhyme is foiled, playfully rather than painfully, by 'clumsy', and unpredictability is maintained when the adjectives find their noun in the faint eroticism of 'dalliance with night'. This eroticism is appropriate: fireflies' lights are often mating signals.

The mating of verbal opposites is a recurrent device. That un-showy oxymoron, 'soothing restlessness', provokes a 'yes, of course'. Watching creatures busy in their creaturely worlds produces an absorbed stillness rather than nervousness in the human watcher. Later, we get 'convivial singleness' and, before that, 'tentative frolic' – an oxymoron with chutzpah. Here, there's extra pleasure from the fact that the dactylic word 'tentative' sounds frolicsome, and the trochaic 'frolic' sounds curt and sober. The dart and exchange of sounds and meanings suggest mating-rituals which, whether of humans or beetles, are often both risky and playful. All 'yet-to-be' projects tend to begin that way, of course, writing poems included.

Despite the surrounding darkness (historical and cosmic, no doubt, as well as local) and occasional sombre notes ('disappointment', 'loneliness'), nothing the fireflies can 'say' or mean is malign. As 'fugitive selves' they represent our best and lightest moments. Even the faintly sinister 'might-have-beens' get an exclamation mark and, being only 'flickery', and given their skippy rhythm, seem to know their place.

The fireflies begin to go their various ways from line 20, after the big questions that have contained their own happy answers. The dark without them has a primitive quality, signalled by the archetypes, 'Chaos and Old Night'. Do the capital letters elevate or debunk those ancient monsters? Perhaps both. But the poem refuses to let go of the hope the fireflies conjured up. The 'absence' which must be the subject of the concluding lines is now marked by remembered, recent brightness and creative possibility. 'Core' is a word that suggests the formation of the earth. The word 'fireflies' recurs in the last line, by means of a rhetorical device known as polyptoton (the same word playing a different part-of-speech) and it's as if the earth were still being formed and transformed, 'brushed by fireflies' wings'. The verb 'brushed' carries delicate tactile hints, including the arts of calligraphy and painting. It might be a little heavy-handed of me, but I'm tempted also to interpret this near-redemption from 'long blackout' as an allusion to Ulster, its war-darkened past, the Good Friday Agreement, and the political renewal we must hope is still evolving.

https://www.theguardian.com/books/2011/dec/19/ poem-of-the-week-fireflies-frank-ormsby

ACKNOWLEDGEMENTS

Thank you to all the poets in this collection, and to the many more who have put on their body-armour and contributed their poems over the years. Thank you *Guardian* people: Sarah Crown, Claire Armistead, Richard Lea, Sian Cain among others. Special thanks to Lindesay Irvine, whose eye for the solecism I very, very occasionally commit is equal to his eye for the appropriate picture each week. Thank you to all the publishers, particularly their publicity departments and poetry editors. And, of course, thank you to Carcanet's Michael Schmidt, whose idea this anthology was, and to Andrew Latimer for all his extra help and hard work.

It would be impossible to list all the contributors to the POTW discussions over the years. But I wanted to mention a few, both in gratitude, and, in some cases, to celebrate the inventiveness and intrigue of a good pseudonym. So I've picked a 'cast in order of appearance' from a single blog, the most recent before *Smart Devices* went to press: the discussion of Zohar Atkins's 'The Oy of the Poyem: 28 Lessons in non-Mastery'. Most of the following are regulars: a couple have never been seen before or since. Thank you, all! IdowuOmoyele, sheenaghpugh, MachenBach, deadgod, roola, gardinergreen, reenimus, nosuchzone, Oudtshoorn, creel, ID5577, thinkfirstactsecond, CCCubon, CharlesBaudelaire, Doshiba, Fromibizatothebroads, theliquidshadow, Xhosa, SoaringSkys, BillyMills, RO42, LesGoodwin, Forgetit, Alarming, gullibletraveller.

Thank you to all the poets, publishers and estates who kindly gave permission for their poems to appear in this anthology:

Altmann, Howard, 'The Lake of Memories' from *In the House* (Turtle Point Press) © Howard Altmann

Anghelaki-Rooke, Katerina, tr. KA-R and Jackie Willcox, 'The Barber Shop' from *The Scattered Papers of Penelope: New and Selected Poems* (Carcanet) © Katerina Anghelaki-Rooke

Ashbery, John, 'Breezeway' from *Breezeway* (Carcanet) © The estate of John Ashbery

Atkins, Zohar, 'The Oy of the Poyem', from *Nineveh* (Carcanet) © Zohar Atkins

Balakian, Peter, 'World Trade Center / Mail Runner / '73' from *Ziggurat* (The University of Chicago Press) © Peter Balakian

Bolam, Robyn, 'Moving On' from *Hyem* (Bloodaxe, 2017) © Robyn Bolam

Bonnefoy, Yves, tr. John Naughton, 'The Light, Changed' from *Collected Poems: 1* (Carcanet) © The estate of Yves Bonnefoy

Breeze, Jean 'Binta', 'Tweet Tweet' from *The Verandah Poems* (Bloodaxe) © Jean 'Binta' Breeze

Burrows, Miles, 'But Those Unheard' from *Waiting for the Nightingale* (Carcanet) © Miles Burrows

Booker, Malika, 'Sin Visits Me' from *Pepper Seed* (Peepal Tree Press) © Malika Booker

Campbell, Siobhan, 'Origin of the Mimeo' from *Heat Signature* (Seren) © Siobhan Campbell

Capildeo, Vahni, 'They (may forget (their names (if let out)))' from *Venus as a Bear* (Carcanet) © Vahni Capildeo

Cheney-Coker, Syl, 'The Colour of Stones' from *The Road to Jamaica, Poems, 1968–1970, and New Poems, 2012–2013* (Karantha Publishing House) © Syl Cheney-Soker

Chowdhry, Maya, 'Microbial Museum' from *Fossil* (Peepal Tree Press) © Maya Chowdhry

Chuilleanáin, Eiléan Ní, 'The Words Collide' from *The Boys From Bluehill* © Eiléan Ní Chuilleanáin

Cogan, Ross, 'Lapstrake', from *Bragr* (Seren) © Ross Cogan

Conran, Tony, 'Jasper' from *Eros Proposes a Toast: Collected Public Poems and Gifts* (Seren) © Tony Conran

D'Aguiar, Fred, 'Boy Soldier' from *The Rose of Toulouse* (Carcanet) © Fred D'Aguiar

Das, Kamala, 'Someone Else's Song' from *Selected Poems* (Penguin Books India) © Kamela Das

Davis, Dick, 'Political Asylum' from *Love in Another Language: Collected Poems and Selected Translations* (Carcanet) © Daick Davis

Didsbury, Peter, 'A Fire Shared' (Bloodaxe) © Peter Didsbury

Eusuf, Nausheen, 'Poem for Professor Frye' from *Not Elegy but Eros* (NQ/BLB) © Nausheen Eusuf

Fainlight, Ruth, 'The Coloration of Feathers', from *Burning Wire* (Bloodaxe) © Ruth Fainlight

Feinstein, Elaine, 'April Fools' Day: In Memory of Isaac Rosenberg' from *Portraits* (Carcanet) © Elaine Feinstein

Forshaw, Cliff, 'Loop' from *Tiger* (HappenStance Press); also in *Vandemonian* (Arc) © Cliff Forshaw

Foyle, Naomi, 'Your Summer Arm' from *The Night Pavilion* (Waterloo Press) © Naomi Foyle

Fried, Philip, 'Yoga for Leaders and Others' from *Squaring the Circle* (Salmon Publishing) © Philip Fried

Fritz, Leah, 'Going, Going…', from *Whatever Sends the Music Into Time* (Salmon Poetry) © Leah Fritz

Gregson, Ian, 'Squawks and Speech' from *How We Met* (Salt) © Ian Gregson

Graham, W.S., 'How Are the Children Robin', from *Implements in their Places* and included in *New Collected Poems* (Faber) © The estate of W.S. Graham

Hacker, Marilyn, 'A Braid of Garlic' from *Names* (W.W. Norton) © Marilyn Hacker

Henry, Paul, 'The Black Guitar', from *The Brittle Sea* (Seren) © Paul Henry

Horta, Maria Teresa, tr. Lesley Saunders, 'Poem' (Stephen Spender Competition, 2016) © Maria Teresa Horta

Kapos, Martha, 'A Mind of Winter' from *Supreme Being* (Enitharmon) © Martha Kapos

Khalvati, Mimi, 'Everywhere you see her…' from *Entries on Light* (Carcanet) © Mimi Khalvati

Kinsella, John, 'Chainsaw' from *Drowning in Wheat: Selected Poems* (Picador) © John Kinsella

Koh, Jee Leong, 'In his Other House' (ref. Ni Chuilleanain) from *Steep Tea* (Carcanet) © Jee Leong Koh

Kunial, Zaffar, 'Us' from *Us* (Faber) © Zaffar Kunial

Lambeth, Andrew, 'Why the Swan?' from *Strix* #5 © Andrew Lambeth

Langley, R.F., 'To a Nightingale', *Complete Poems* (Carcanet)

Lewis, Saunders, 'Lavernock' tr. Harry Gilonis: Welsh text from *Sirwan a Cherddi Eraille* (Abertawe C. Davies); English translation published as a Form Books Formcard, reproduced by permission of the author.

Mills, Billy, 'Tiny Pieces' from *Lares, Manes: Collected Poems* (Shearsman) © Billy Mills

Morgan, Edwin, Vladimir Mayakovsky 'Aye, but can ye?' from *Collected Translations* (Carcanet) © The estate of Edwin Morgan

Moss, Stanley, 'Visiting Star' from *It's About Time* (Carcanet) © Stanley Moss

Nash, Mirian, 'Walking Father Blues' from *All the Prayers in the House* (Bloodaxe) © Miriam Nash

Ormsby, Frank, 'Fireflies', from *Fireflies* (Carcanet) © Frank Ormsby

Riley, Denise, 'Death makes dead metaphor revive', from *Say Something Back* (Picador) © Denise Riley
Rutherford, Maurice, 'The Autumn Outings' from *And Saturday is Christmas* (Shoestring) © Maurice Rutherford
Sheppard, Robert, 'Prison Camp Violin, Riga', from *History or Sleep: Selected Poems* (Shearsman) © Robert Sheppard
Stevenson, Anne, 'The Miracle of the Bees and the Foxgloves', *Astonishment* (Bloodaxe) © Anne Stevenson
Willson, Judith, 'A Bone Flute', *Crossing the Mirror Line* (Carcanet) © Judith Wilson
Woolf, Karen McCarthy, 'Outside' from *Seasonal Disturbances* (Carcanet) © Karen McCarthy Woolf
Yeh, Jane, 'Musk Ox' from *The Ninjas* (Carcanet) © Jane Yeh

INDEX OF POEM TITLES